THE TEN DECISIVE BATTLES OF CHRISTIANITY

The Ten Decisive Battles of Christianity

By

FRANK SPENCER MEAD

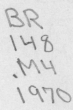

BR
148
.M4
1970

Essay Index Reprint Series

 BOOKS FOR LIBRARIES PRESS
FREEPORT, NEW YORK

INTERNATIONAL STANDARD BOOK NUMBER:

0-8369-1812-6

LIBRARY OF CONGRESS CATALOG CARD NUMBER:

72-117823

PRINTED IN THE UNITED STATES OF AMERICA

CONTENTS

THE TEN DECISIVE BATTLES OF CHRISTIANITY

I

THE RESURRECTION

A CLAY-COLD wind moaned 'round the hill, and clouds of furious black drove down the sky like chariots out of hell, with the devil's fiends driving. Demons on holiday, they frightened the earth; the watchers on the hill pretended not to see or hear or be afraid, but the housewives of Jerusalem drew their shutters and barred their doors and sat pale at their supper-tables, listening. A sense of doom, of death, was in the air. For love was in eclipse this night, and hope hung lifeless on a cross atop the hill. Jesus Christ was dead.

Two men moved warily up the infinite ascent, their shoulders hunched against the evil wind, their faces half concealed, bearing between them a burden of aloes and myrrh, of linen bands and a clean white winding-sheet and a writ from Pontius Pilate. They were alien to such a scene as this; they were high-born, aristocrats, Sanhedrinists; they were rich Joseph of Arimathea and Nicodemus, friend of night. They drew their robes closer as they passed the ditch where lay the bodies of the two dead thieves, twisted grotesquely in death's cold pantomime; they nodded the sad mourner's nod to the three Marys at the cross. The Marys did not see them, or reply. Mary the Mother was prostrate on the ground, quiet at last in the merciful exhaustion of bitter grief. Mary the mother of James knelt near her, speechless, comfortless, as much afraid for her disciple son as grieving for this Son upon the tree. Above them stood Mary of Magdala, hands pressed to her temples, eyes fixed in the wild stare of a frightened doe, mute, bewildered, wondering why God's chariots had not come. For the Magdalene, who had leaped from lowest earth to sweetest Heaven at the touch of those pierced hands, did not yet believe it. But the two newcomers believed it. With eyes more human than Mary's, they searched out the Roman ladder, placed it carefully against the cross, and prepared without a word to take the body down.

Even Jesus could never have suspected these two would come with Pilate's writ to claim his body; they were the most improbable burying-party in all Jerusalem. John the Beloved might have come, for John stood with Mother Mary while He died; but John may have loved too much to venture the awful task. Peter might have volunteered, but Peter was in another funk of faithlessness. Doubting Thomas might have tried it, in tardy penance for his doubt; but Thomas's doubts were now confirmed, and somewhere in the black blanket of the night he was saying, "I told you so." Even Judas might have offered, in atonement for his ghastly bargaining, but Judas was more terribly dead than Jesus. There were the other disciples—Luke, James, Philip, Thaddeus, Mark—but who could find them? They had scattered like sheep as the Shepherd fell, seeking holes in which to hide from grim Roman and weasel Pharisee. Hence, these two Sanhedrinists, who were not disciples, who had feared to condemn Him in the council lest their hands be stained with His blood. Now they came and drew the nails and filled the wounds with spice while the blood of the slain Lamb fell on their hands, their arms, their faces, their errant feet. They knew now, if they did not know before, that this blood had been shed for them, and they were not ashamed of it nor fearful of its stain.

Down into Joseph's garden they bore the body of their

friend, reverently washed and placed the pierced limbs, gently folded the torn hands that in life had tried to lift them, sorrowfully closed the lips that living had spoken words that could never die. The Marys added perfume and tears to the aloes and the myrrh, wound the napkins and stood away as the men bore the body into the flickering torchlight of the tomb. It was Joseph's tomb, built by himself against the day of his own death. He did not think of that now. All that mattered now was that this body should be saved from the common ditch of the thieves, that it be safely in the tomb before the dawn of the Sabbath, as the law commanded. With the aid of the two Roman guards, they rolled a giant stone, or slab, to close the gaping door. The Sanhedrinists recited the Hebrew psalm for the dead, stood about a moment in agonized futility, and went down at last toward the waning lights of cruel and doomed Jerusalem.

They went, but not the women; these stood like black statues, rooted in the garden rock. They pressed their hands against the rock; they called, and He did not answer. The guards did not rebuke them. Said one: "Fools! Don't they know the man is dead? Why don't they go home?" Said the other, who had a son in a tomb near River Tiber: "Home, my comrade? It is home no longer, but a torture-house where livid memory holds the keys, where they shall think they hear His footfall on the stair, where they shall wait hushed for His knock upon the door." He dropped two sticks into his fire, and started as he noticed they burned in the shape of a fiery cross.

But spent at last, even the women crept away, as the first long gleam of the dawn pierced the darkness like the rising white finger of God. Before it, with one last roll of thunder, hell's charioteers fled in tumult from the sky. Their work was done. For this one night at least, they had captured the world, and as they fled they took as hostages the hopes of those who loved the Lord and put their faith in God. The next day was the Sabbath, the Passover Sabbath, and all rested. That is, they did nothing. What was there to do? All was over. The debacle was complete. This Jesus had bowed His head and given up the ghost; with His own lips He had cried, "It is finished!" Everything was finished. Roman nails had ended Him, after all; He was human; He died as all men die; He had failed. No failure in all history had ever been so convincing, so shatteringly convincing and complete, as the failure of Jesus on that Passover Sabbath; no symbol of failure was ever so eloquent as that bleak cross on Calvary's brow. He could not save Himself from that, though He had saved others from worse; He could not call down his Father's angels to help, though He had made angels seem as real as men to those who followed Him. He was not a King, after all; those who loved Him had been deceived as to His nature. His "kingdom" lay in ruins; it was a candle blown out, a bubble pricked by Roman spears. Just another dreamer who had had a pretty dream, who had given the world one more false hope: a Platonic Utopia plus a new God, but like all others, just . . . Utopia. He was too impractical. He could never win. Cæsar and swords were the rulers of earth, not God or love or brotherhood. Cæsar had not even heard of Jesus Christ; Pilate had already forgotten Him. The world about Jerusalem dropped back into its timeless rut, knowing now that this effort of Jesus was but a capricious interlude in the struggle of the fittest to survive. The rabbis and the Sanhedrinists were gesturing again, like the automatons that they were, over their basins of blood and through their ineffective ritual and cant; the legionnaires in barracks had an extra cup of wine. The disciples crouched in the shadows, daring not to face the light of day, knowing not at all what to do with themselves, the moment, or tomorrow; their disillusionment had sponged away the last memory of His words, "On the third day I will rise. . . ." He was dead. And Christianity was dead. Dead as Alexander or the Golden Age. It was finished. Everything was finished.

Yet there is no night so densely dark but that in it some eye may catch the gleam of a distant star, or some hope hear the rustle of an angel's wing. At the dawn of the next day, four women came from the city to the tomb. Why? "To anoint Him," says Mark; to finish the hasty anointing of Good Friday night. They came in obedience to custom. And, one loves to think, at the behest of hope. They may not have been quite sure (as women never are) that the dead are forever gone when they cross the Stygian gulf; they may have dared to hope they would find more in Joseph's garden than a tomb, and guards, and a seal. But they were practical about it; as they walked they asked one another, "Who shall roll us away the stone from the door of the Sepulchre?" Four women. The last four to give up, the first four to return to the scene of mankind's superlative crime. Joanna, and Salome, and Mary the widow of Clopas; and Mary the Magdalene. Which saw it first?

Which one of these four brains or hearts saw first just what had happened there? Which eye first saw the open door, the stone rolled away? Who led the rush to the tomb's entrance, where they stood like children come suddenly on a forest cave, not daring to trespass farther than the door but longing to, with all that is within them? There they stood. There the great news burst upon them: *the body was gone!*

[15]

All the wonderings and calculations, all the glib and hasty explanations of twenty subsequent centuries leaped to the minds of these four women as they peered into the heart of that dim and empty tomb. Someone had stolen it, some thief. Some hired thief of the enemies of Jesus, who had added the crowning infamy of hurling it into the ditch of the thieves. Or His friends had stolen out, overcome the guards and moved the remains of their Redeemer to some spot Rome could never find, nor the wolves of the synagogue ever violate. Or He had not been really dead when they placed Him there; He had torn loose from the bands and the winding-sheet, eluded the guards and escaped into Galilee, where He might hide in some fisher's hut. They thought of all this. They did not think, they did not know that they were the first to arrive on the first great battlefield of the Christian faith, where the risen Master was to struggle to make Himself known, to make Himself real in the eyes and lives of all who beheld Him. They did not remember that He had promised to arise.

There lay the napkin, neatly folded; there lay the winding-sheet, not rent nor torn, but whole, carefully laid aside. The silence of the place pounded at their ears like close thunder. And it came to them that in this place, when they had entered it, that they were not alone. The sepulchre was not empty; there were unearthly beings here, two young men arrayed in garments of gleaming white, like angel-garments, sitting on that shelf of rock where they had left the body of the Lord. And one of the young men spoke and asked of them: "Why seek ye the living among the dead?" Aye, why? Why do we still hover over graves in cemeteries, thinking loved ones are there? Why do we believe we shall find the living moving among the dark palaces of the merely physically dead? Why? "He is not here, but He is risen! . . . Ye shall see Him. . . . Go, tell the disciples and Peter. . . ." They backed from the voice, stiff with terror. They did not scream, for they could not. They reached the door, gave back one final reasonless, insensate stare, and they turned and ran. They did not gather up their skirts; they did not pick their way across the garden, through the bramble and the stones; they only ran in maniacal heedlessness, away from there. Away! Hands outstretched before them, hands clutched, though they could not feel it, by the hands of that guardian angel of all who fear, who led them straight in their terror to tell the disciples . . . and Peter.

The Magdalene told Peter. He was with John. Breathless, she burst into their hideaway, and cried that "they" had taken away the body of their Lord, and hidden it she knew not where. And Peter stared at her first and then smiled, for he thought her mind was gone. And John pitied her with his soft mystic's eyes; John thought she had loved this Nazarene even more than had he, too deeply, too much. But when she insisted, when she paced the floor and tore at her veil and scratched at her eyes, then they arose and went out to the tomb to satisfy her . . . and themselves. They were not satisfied. Peter rushed in, with that impetuosity that was as much a part of him as breathing and wild boast, and he saw the folded linen and the body gone, and no more. John stood stunned, with the truth knocking at his heart's door, announcing to him the Resurrection. But the heart's door did not open; John went away with Peter, both of them "wondering at that which had come to pass," still unconvinced.

They left the Magdalene behind them, weeping in the garden. She sat as one already dead, her eyes set rigidly, her mind a fever. Gone! They had even stolen His body! And no man would tell her where. . . . A shadow fell across her shoulder and a voice came: "Woman, why weepest thou?" It was the gardener, she told herself; she glanced at the shadow, no further. And it was the question of a fool. She answered him shortly: "Sir, if *you* have taken Him hence, tell me. . . ." The voice came again, and it was this time a voice that seemed to come to her from the other side of the garden wall, or from behind the stars or back of the sun. Wistfully, longingly, surfeited with pathos and tears yet light and lovely as the lilies at her feet and clear as the tinkling of a silver bell, it was one word: "Mary!" Her eye raced up the shadow to the face, and she flung herself full length upon the grass. The first decisive battle of the risen Christ against the doubt of the world had been won; the first believer uttered but one low word: "Master!"

Again she burst in upon the disciples. Now she did not pace the floor nor tear her veil. Now she stood transfixed, transformed, speaking in a dazed undertone, speaking words that fell like the soft notes of a muted violin: "I have seen Him." Again they smiled. Again they turned from her to their mournful meat, to talk among themselves of her condition. These women! The tales they tell. Idle tales. Gossip. Dreams. Hallucinations. The hysteria of the weak. Nerves. Reaction following shock. Women were weak and they, the men, were strong. They were not fooled. They debated among themselves as to who might have stolen the body. And Mary retired to a dark corner from whence she cried, at intervals in their childish debate: "But I tell you, I have seen Him. He *spoke* to me. He lives." She knew it. Whatever they said, she knew it. There was a singing in her blood and a shout in her soul: "He lives!"

Meanwhile the shadow fell again, across the road to Emmaus; across the path of two travelers out of Jerusalem. Two men not disciples, arguing about the crucifixion, and the tomb, and Him. They did not know Him as they walked together into the town; they did not know Him as He sat down to sup with them. But when He reached across the table to break the bread, they saw the nail-prints, and they knew. They rushed back to Jerusalem crying, "He lives! We have seen Him."

Ten of the disciples were come together in a room in Jerusalem; they were ten who must be won, who must see and know this Risen One if His gospel were to be given to the world, if there were to be a Church to carry on. To them He came; across their table the shadow fell. Their door was barred and their windows were locked, yet the shadow fell. In their midst they sensed His presence. They would not believe it. He showed them His wounded hands and side, yet they dispersed, went back to fish in the sea and trade in the marketplace, supposing "that they had beheld a Spirit."

They told their vision to Thomas called Didymus, prince of this world's doubters, and Thomas shook his head. "Except I see in his hands the print of the nails . . . I will not believe." For eight days he would not believe; then the marching shadow fell across his path, and he heard a voice saying, "Thomas, reach hither thy hand, and put it into my side." The Doubter could not lift his hand, but his lips framed the words: "My Lord, and my God!" And Thomas had been won before the rest of the Band!

Seven disciples had returned to fish in Galilee, forgetful that they had promised to fish for men. In the cool of the dawn a voice came sweet and low across the still waters:

[19]

"Children, have ye aught to eat?" Have you caught any-thing? Are you happy here, and successful? They had not caught a single fish; they caught a bursting netful when He told them to cast their nets on the other side, and John cried out, "It is the Lord;" and Peter leaped into the lake and swam ashore. Ashore they heard Him say, "Feed my sheep. . . . Follow me." And they fed and followed; they never returned to their Galilean nets again, but roamed the earth casting their nets for men, and reaping such a harvest that all the world marveled. The crisis was over when Peter leaped out of that boat: he and his fellow fishermen were on their way to us with the stupendous statement that there is no death and that Jesus called the Christ is with us even unto the end of the world.

Omar the Persian has an oft-quoted line: "The moving finger writes, and having writ moves on . . ."; Christ im-proved on that when He wrote, with His moving shadow, across the lives of men the fact that He was risen. He wrote it across a mountain, where five hundred were gathered, where they saw and believed, where they heard Him say to His disciples: "Go ye therefore, and make disciples of all nations." He wrote it into the life of his own Brother James, who was to become the leader of the Apostolic Church. He wrote it across the lives of hundreds more who saw Him ere he ascended to His Father, hundreds who told thousands. The thousands told more thousands. About Jerusalem and down every Judean dusty road the good news flashed: "He lives." It crashed every skeptic's door: "He has come back." Into Pilate's palace and Herod's throne-room and into the cote of the beggar came the tidings: "Jesus Christ is risen from the dead!" The world of flesh halted in amazement and asked itself: "Can it be there is no death?" Lost, overwhelmed in the triumph of the Resurrection truth was the ageless question of smitten Job and smitten mankind: "If a man die, shall he live again?" Man and the ages had their answer: "This Man lives."

Why do we call it *the* resurrection? There were three resurrections here. There was the resurrection of a Man, of an Individual. One who wore our flesh came back from the other side. In that same flesh He had come out of that shadow-land from whence no man before Him had ever returned; and coming, He gave to men the knowledge that like Him they should rise. As it was with Him, so was it to be with us: "Let not your heart be troubled: . . . because I live, ye shall live also." In all the words of all the men that ever lived there is nothing to equal it; in all the ages and in all the world there has never been a hope that meant so much as this: *we cannot die.* Tides have risen in the affairs of men, calamity and joy o'erwhelmed us, yet after all has happened we have risen to struggle on with that one challenge to failure and pain and death upon us: *we cannot die.* Murderers climbing the scaffold and saints in their clean white beds; men who have trod the ways of life in company with God and men who have walked alone have put their last trust in Him who crossed the gulf before them and waits there with outstretched hand to help them across. Paul says it all for us when he says, "This mortal must put on immortality;" not "this mortal would like to," or "it would be nice if this mortal could"; but it is in the imperative mood: "this mortal *must.*" From out the tomb in Joseph's garden there came the hope of the individual; when He walked from that garden back into the world, He was blazing for the centuries the path from one world, one life, to another. But for that walking, we would still think of the grave as the dismal end of

the dismal road of life, and not as a golden door. He made
of death, for us, life's most beautiful adventure.

There was the resurrection of a Spirit. "And I will pray
the Father, and He shall give you another Comforter, that
he may abide with you forever; even the Spirit of Truth."
Not only did Man come forth, but a Spirit which was truth,
the truth which was very God incarnate in the Man. Christ
said the world would not "receive" it; how well He knew!
The world has rebelled against the presence of that truth;
the world has flouted it, tried to hide it, hissed, hooted,
sneered, spurned it, tried to burn, strangle, smother, stab and
slay it; the world has turned from one martyr stake to the
next, from that one to discover the truth lodged in the breast
of another man. "Truth forever on the scaffold, Wrong forever on the throne." Who said that? Who was so deluded?
Truth has forever come down from the scaffold, bearing an
eternal reprieve, and wrong has never held its grip for long
on any throne. Man has moved, however slowly, from transient error to obedience to this spirit of God's truth, from
the cruelties of barbarism to justice and a larger mercy in
Christian civilization. And it has come every step of the way
with Christ in the van, a living, risen, deathless Christ whom
we cannot put away. A great poet sings:

> "The Christ, Whose friends have played Him false,
>   Whom dogmas have belied,
> Still speaking of the hearts of men—tho' shamed
>   and crucified,
> The Master of the centuries, Who will not be denied."

But the greatest of the resurrections was the resurrection
of Christianity, of that organized faith which has kept alive
for nineteen hundred years the news that its Leader con-

quered death. The most amazing fact here is not that Jesus rose, but that the certain knowledge of that rising completely transformed the life of every man and woman who accepted it. Cowards, caught in the Great Conviction, became heros loving death, begging for it, if it were to be death for Christ's sake. It made of sinful Mary Magdalene a saint for whom we are proud to name our churches. It changed Peter from a reed swaying in every least wind to an immortal who was truly rock. It took eleven men once ashamed to own their Lord and made of them zealots who laughed at the threats of Pilate and the crosses of Rome and who were so convinced that they won three thousand for Christ in a single day! It brought forth from the shadows of Jerusalem a Church crippled in infancy, disillusioned, leaderless, broken, and made it a Church mighty enough to upset the world and toy with Empires and set the course of Western history.

Fools still prate of how the resurrection "might be explained"; they are sparrows fighting falcons, flickering candles defying the sun. Why waste one's life at that? Why waste one precious minute? The Marys at the tomb had all the doubts and explanations that any of us have ever had; we have not added a single, solitary one. When some prater, some explainer explains to us how that resurrection became objectified in the minds of His followers, he will be doing something worthy of intelligent attention.

French Renan "explained" everything from Bethlehem to Calvary in three hundred pages. Says Renan at the end of his honeyed words: "For the historian, the life of Jesus ends with his last sigh." God pity him, that's where the Life begins, *and where history begins.* History since Golgotha has been made by those who have kept their eyes upon His shining head. Take that one head, that one face away, and there is no explaining what we have become. Take the resurrection out of the record of Jesus, and all the rest is idle talk; take it out of Christianity and there would be no Christianity at all. And if no Christianity, no Church.

The tomb rivals the manger, the resurrection contests the claim of the birth as God's great boon to man. It has made us see life as never-ending, as eternal, as a pilgrimage and not as a fiercely futile struggle for existence ending in the darkness of the grave. It has put before us a Principle, a Spirit, even the Spirit of God's truth, set like a star for the ship of civilization to steer by, to set her course by. And it has placed at the helm of that ship an institution, an organization of that truth, whose business it has been, is and ever shall be to hold the ship steady, to guide it through the storms and strifes of men, with the aid and counsel of a deathless Captain to safe haven. The haven we call the Kingdom of God, and it is civilization's goal. The Captain is the risen Christ, and without His presence we should long since have foundered and gone down.

II

THE COUNCIL OF JERUSALEM

PAUL was a preaching fugitive, hovering about the horizons of Jerusalem like a vagrant cloud, disappearing, reappearing, never quite gone, preaching and running and returning to preach again. His own, his brother Jews, pursued him; once his friends, they were now become the bloodhounds of the affrighted rulers, baying at his heels; sometimes these went before him as the agents of misinformation, to undermine him and turn the crowd against him ere he rose to preach. They feared him, and because they feared, they hated him. He had been one of them, a Hebrew of the Hebrews, a Pharisee and the son of a Pharisee, an authority on that code of codes on which all things Jewish were built: the Mosaic Law. And he had left them, turned his back on them and their law, denied them for a crucified carpenter, backslider, renegade deserter. Out with him. Down with him. Beat him with lictor's rods, stone him, kill him, anything to be rid of him. He was Jewry's anathema.

His old friends hated him, and his new friends were suspicious of him. The Apostles and the elders in the mother Church at Jerusalem were a little disturbed over his easy ways with the heathen. He was taking droves of pagans into the Church; he had established whole churches composed exclusively of Gentiles, who were jubilant over Christ but who ignored the Law; he was doing this without their permission, without even consulting them. What right had he to do that?

Were not the men of Jerusalem the acknowledged leaders of Christ's new Church? Had not these Apostles walked with the Master, received their commission direct from Him? Whence came Paul's commission? He had not been with Jesus; he had been an enemy of Jesus, a henchman of the Pharisees, standing idly and approvingly by while Stephen the Martyr died. But now he went about his preaching as though he had spent his whole life with the Lord, as certain of his right and calling to preach as any Apostle. The Apostles, to be sure, were lenient with him, and brotherly; but there was a sect of Christian Pharisees in the Jerusalem Church that frowned upon him. Who was he to act in this high-handed way? Where were his credentials? Where had he been ordained? They wanted to know. Paul told them. He told them Christ had sent him forth, even as he had sent the Apostles. "Have I not seen Jesus Christ our Lord?" On the road to Damascus, face to face? Do you doubt that credential, brethren? He was "an apostle not of men, neither by man, but by Jesus Christ and God the Father." Did they doubt that? And did they doubt that he was doing wonders for Christ among the Gentiles? No, they could find no fault with that. It is always hard to find fault with those who, "improperly" ordained, have succeeded where the "properly" ordained have failed.

Circled in by hateful enemy and suspicious brother, Paul plunged on; he steered his course between the Scylla of the Synagogue and the Charybdis of the Christian Judaizers; he went preaching through Jerusalem, Damascus and Antioch. He had a good time of it at Antioch; he mustered there the first Foreign Legion of the Church, a legion made up of Jews, Hellenists and Greeks, a church so strong that it became the mother Church of Gentile Christianity, as the Jerusalem

Church was the mother Church of the Christian Jew. Antioch was headquarters; he worked out from there into the Gentile country, without orders from Jerusalem; he was so effective among the Gentiles that he had come to think of himself as having a special mission among them, as set apart for them. The Jews wouldn't listen to him. They had cast him out. All right, he would preach to those who would listen: to the non-Jews. He took Barnabas and set out on his first missionary tour; they went like Abraham, not knowing whither they went, nor what awaited them there, and not caring. For God went with them, as with Father Abraham. . . .

They preached in Paphos, and there confounded a false prophet; they exhorted in Perga of Pamphylia and in Pisidian Antioch and in the cities of Lycaonia, that land that was a dreary plain bare of trees and destitute of water. They passed through that desert and left it blooming, left it filled with singing Gentiles who drank deep of the living water from Antioch. They back-tracked along their trail, preaching a second time in the cities they had touched (a feat courageous for any evangelist) and turned happily home, two tired conquerors, to report to headquarters. They hurried; their step was light in the knowledge of great things done and in the knowledge that Antioch would rejoice. Antioch rejoiced . . . with half a heart. The missionaries looked at each other. Something had happened in Antioch while they had been away. Something disturbing. A snake had crawled into Eden.

The "snake" was a delegation of agitators from that sect of Christian Pharisees at Jerusalem. They had come to talk to the Gentiles about the Law; they had come as Jews first and as Christian brothers second. Why not? They could come no other way, inasmuch as they thought of Christianity as an extension of Judaism. They talked softly to the Gentiles of Antioch, telling them that they must be circumcized and obey the Law in every last and little detail. For the Law of Moses was the beginning and the end of faith and life. Take away Moses and his precepts, and what was left? It meant to them what the Constitution means to a good American, what the King means to the Englishman. Yes, the Law was long, complex, bewildering, but it must be kept faithfully if salvation were desired. Why, the Law itself declared that man accursed and damned who did not keep the *whole* Law, every bit of it, every last word of it. Every convert in Antioch must obey it, rigidly. This carelessness must stop!

Above all, all Antiochenes must be circumcised. That was the mark of loyalty, the sign of those true to the faith. No Christian was a Christian without it; even Jesus had been circumcized, and James and Peter and John, and Paul! What are you thinking of, Antioch, to neglect this? Do you think we in Jerusalem, in the first Church, will tolerate it? You must be circumcized, immediately, or you are no part of us. If you want to be Christians, you must first be . . . Jews! They read the words of the Law on that, over and over and over; they pounded their law-books; they talked incessantly of Moses and Abraham; they poured forth tears of burning rage and words as soft as silk. Would Antioch deny the fathers of Israel, the fathers of Christ? Would Antioch blaspheme? Would Antioch dare leave the beaten path? For shame, Gentiles! Mend your ways, and quickly, or you are lost. There is no middle path, no other way. The Judaizers from Jerusalem were firm about it.

And the Gentiles were furious. They loathed circumcision. To them, it was a disgusting ritual, and they would have none of it, whatever happened. And the Law? What could that mean to them? They had lived without it, thus far, and they felt they hadn't missed anything. They were interested not in Moses but in Christ, not in dead yesterdays but in vibrant tomorrows; not in binding themselves in the toils of an ancient Law but in freeing themselves through Christ. They told the Judaizers that, in plain terms, and the Judaizers screamed and shouted of the Law, the Law, the Law. Bedlam reigned; Babel was rebuilt, and another confusion of tongues was upon them. Gentle Barnabas tried to halt the storm, but no one heard him; Paul met fire with fire: "The just shall live by faith, and the Law is not of faith!" The world wasn't going to be saved by lock-stepping through the Law, but by faith in Christ. The letter killeth, but the spirit giveth life. Paul loved the Law as much as they; he honored it until he died. But he had met something greater than the Law on the highroad to Damascus. He tried to explain that, but they wouldn't listen, wouldn't try to understand. There they stood, stubborn, immovable, at the impasse. It was a church fight and a bad one. Paul saw in a flash that unless the breach were healed, the Church would be split in two: there would be one church for the Jew, with its capital at Jerusalem, and one for the Gentiles, at Antioch. One organized on the Law, one without it. They would be friendly enemies, and their mutual enemy would laugh at them. That must not happen, said Paul. He called a meeting.

The meeting agreed that something had to be done; race riots and civil war were all too often the outcome of such troubles as this, and they knew from experience that men inflamed in religious passion were the bloodiest of rioters. That could not be, among Christians; they must settle this as Christian gentlemen. The Church must be one, united;

not two, divided. There was too much to be done around Antioch; the whole Gentile world beyond their walls, Gentile and Jewish, Greek, Roman, Scythian, Syrian, must hear of Christ. They must settle their differences to get that done. They did. They sent a delegation to Jerusalem to talk it over, or talk it out, with the Apostles and the elders. They sent Paul and Barnabas, and Titus, and some others. They did not realize what they were doing. They did not know that they had brought about the First Council of the Christian Church, that they were forcing a decision on the most momentous question ever to face that Church, that they were pushing Paul up to the door that led out to the Gentile world and helping him to hold it open, on howsoever tiny a crack, for Christ to pass through. Had they not done as they did and sent that delegation, Christianity today would be the property of a dwindling sect in Jerusalem. It might not even be that.

All Antioch turned out the day the delegates left, singing and praying them to the edges of the town, watching from a hilltop as the travelers disappeared in a cloud of dust around a bend in the road. This was Antioch's own Easter; the sun was high and bright and warm and every bush along the wayside was afire with God. This was the day the Lord had made for them. They said in their hearts that Paul and his men would convince the elders and bring Christ back triumphant, freed of the trappings of Judaism, for the whole world to know and love. They went singing back to Antioch and took up the daily task in a fever of hope. Mothers looked down the road as they rocked their cradles: "Where are they tonight?" Men fumbled their tools and told their questing hearts: "They should be at Jerusalem. I wonder what . . ."

Down through Phœnicia and Samaria they go; their entry

into every town is the signal for rejoicing, for every town knows what they are about, knows that upon the outcome of this march on Jerusalem hangs their hope of Christ. The cavalcade is received everywhere with open arms; there are quiet hours of prayer in homes where the travelers stay; there are services in the churches; there are coins slipped into the apostolic hands, and food and water and words of cheer brought forth on the morning of departure. The jeer of the cynical Jew is drowned in the tear of the expectant Gentile; the footfalls of the grim marchers shake the countryside; the stars tremble in their courses.

When they arrived in Jerusalem, tired, hungry, the Apostles and the elders were already met in Council, breathing an air charged with excitement. It was the year 50 A.D. The men of Antioch search out their quarters, the houses of their friends, to rest before the battle. Paul does not rest. He searches out Peter, and James, and John. Where they met that night, no man knows; what they said, we can only approximate. But they met, in secret, and in secret they found common ground. Thus are great decisions arrived at, great events arranged, great conflicts won. Call it strategy, call it politics, call it anything. This way are presidents chosen and revolutions hatched and empires divided and the currents of history turned; by leaders, in secret, before the public conclave. This way, before the Jerusalem Council convened, the men who were to control it set the stage and determined the course of action.

James the Just, the brother of the Lord, presided. He was the man for it: he had the admiration and the love of both sides. He loved the Law. He was a good Jew; some say he was a Nazarite, a celibate, eschewing wine and flesh, letting his hair grow long and wearing neither sandals nor garments of wool. He spent much time in prayer, so much time that his knees were calloused, like a camel's. His title, "The Just," was deserved; he lived justly, and the Council knew, as he sat there in his bright white linen ephod at their head, that his decision would be . . . just. There he sat, Jew of the Jews. There sat Paul with Barnabas, Jew of the Jews too but also schooled in the culture of the Greeks and a citizen of Rome, a man at home anywhere. And there sat the Judaizers, quietly waiting, resolved grimly to have their way. James calls on Paul to report his work. Paul rises, turns and faces the Council.

Have you a picture of him there? We are told he was "small in size, with meeting eyebrows, with a rather large nose, baldheaded, bowlegged, strongly built, full of grace, for at times he looked like a man and at times he had the face of an angel." That description may or may not be true, but that day it was true in at least one respect: that day Paul had grace, and the inspired face of one from another world. He began quietly, telling where he had been and what he had been doing, how he had preached to the Gentiles and how the Gentiles had flocked to him as he upheld the cross. It was a good report; Barnabas added to it, gave more details, made it seem even more wonderful. There was no denying it, these men had done a great work out there among the Gentiles, and . . .

A Judaizer rose, almost screaming: "But they have not been circumcized! They do not keep the Law!" Report or no report, they insisted on that; they wanted that settled, at whatever cost; they threw down the gauntlet, touched the spark to the powder. The whole room seemed to explode. Fierce argument broke out all over the place with the venerable James unable to make himself heard above the confusion. Even Paul could do nothing. But God had an ambassador there who could do something, one sent against this hour, one with the gift of leaping into the thick of any fray and making the fray swirl about him as its center. This one leaped to his feet, and above the hubbub his great voice boomed:

"Brethren!"

The confusion wavered; hot words stopped unspoken on wild tongues, and a sea of faces turned upward toward the voice. It was Peter! Peter, who had struck off the ear of the High Priest's servant, who had leaped into the sea. Peter the impulsive, the impassioned, the outspoken, Peter whose natural habitat was havoc and who feared no man alive.

"Brethren!"

His brave old head soared, riding the tumult of their lesser heads and minds like a fisher-boat riding out a storm on Galilee. The last voice died; eyes that dared not meet the righteous eye of The Rock shifted, looked away; there was a shamed shuffle back to order.

"Brethren, ye know how that a good while ago God made choice amongst us, that the Gentiles by my mouth should hear the word of the gospel, and believe!" You *all* know that; some of you heard Jesus say it, with your own ears; you know I, Peter, converted Cornelius the centurian, and ye said nothing! "And God . . . bare them witness, giving them [the Gentiles] the Holy Ghost, even as he did unto us; and put no difference between us and them, purifying their hearts by faith!" You know that, too; you know Christ told us to go to *all* nations, all men; what makes you think this gospel is yours alone? How dare ye try to hide Christ's light beneath the bushel of your Law? How dare you throw your stumbling-blocks of dead tradition before the feet of His

[33]

disciples? How dare ye hinder the work of God? ". . . why tempt ye God, to put a yoke upon the neck of the disciples, which neither our fathers nor we were able to bear?" The yoke of circumcision! And the yoke of the unbearable Law! Hasn't all that done harm enough, to our fathers who struggled with it; to us? Why are ye so obsessed with this one rite? Why do ye cling to it, seeing it drives all else than Jews away? Ye know we were never saved by circumcision, but by faith! Yet you think the rite more vital than the saving! The method more important than the end! Will ye continue to fuss and mumble through the mechanics of your Law, with a whole world waiting to gain the freedom we have found in Christ? No! "Through the grace of Lord Jesus Christ we shall be saved, even as they." Moses gave you your law and Jesus Christ gave you grace. Choose now, ye of the Council, which ye shall pass on to the ages. Choose!

Every word was a hammer-blow; the room was in stunned silence as Peter sat down. Even the Pharisees were stilled; Peter's eyes had startled them, but his words had burned them. They sat speechless as Paul rose to speak again. Paul and Barnabas, to finish their report. They told of more Gentile conquests, of other wonders Christ had done through them for those who lived beyond the pale. They did not boast. They simply told their story. They told it so calmly, so sincerely, so clearly that the Council forgot the council-room, found itself standing on a curbstone in Paphos hearing Barnabas tell of the Master; they were in Perga, mingling with the Gentile crowd; they were in Pisidian Antioch, watching Paul cast the spell of the Nazarene over a heathen mob. They saw the signs, the wonders, the victories. It was the quiet recital of two men who had done well, who overbalanced pretty theory with a cool record of accomplishment. Thus had Christ wrought in the Gentile heart. Would you stop it, Council? Would you crucify Christ afresh on the Gentile road? Paul finished and sat down, leaving the fate of Christianity as a world religion in their hands. Choose, Council. Choose, now!

There was another silence, which the Judaizers might have broken. None broke it. Perhaps they knew the day was lost for them; perhaps they sensed the fact that now the majority had been won away from them, over to the side of Peter and Paul. There was no further voice, no further argument, and James arose to pronounce his judgment. It was more of gentle suggestion than judgment; he was James the Cautious here, James the Careful, the Compromising. He said a good word for the work of Peter; he said the Old Testament had prophesied that someone like Peter would convert the heathen to Christ, and he quoted the words of Amos to prove it. He did not mention the word "circumcision"; he insinuated by the assent of silence that there was to be no more of it among the Gentiles; he settled that question by the wisest of methods: by not settling it at all, by letting it die a natural death. He suggested to his Jewish brethren that they "trouble not them which from among the Gentiles are turned to God" with such a burden. And he suggested to the Gentiles that they in turn respect the sensibilities and consciences of Jewry by abstaining from idol worship, from things strangled (sacrificial animals from which the blood had not been let), and from blood (the Jews shied from blood, for to them blood was life), and from fornication (from the sex-rituals and the sacred prostitutes who swarmed in heathen temples). In other words, Jews were to be careful not to offend Gentiles, and the Gentiles were to give no offense to

the Jews. It was saying that if the eating of meat offended
a brother, then one should stop eating meat; if a hand
offended, then cut off that hand. Love one another, Christians, even as Christ has loved you. Waste no time disputing
those things unworthy of dispute. Cease contending. You
have work to do. Do it. Do it together. This was a plea for
unity. This was a compromise.

Critics and cranks have called that judgment bad; they
have bewailed the compromise of James the Just, and held
that he should have taken a firmer stand. But time has
proved that James was wise; he took the only stand that
could have saved the day. Had he been "firm" (belligerent)
he would have crashed the Council and the Church on the
rocks of continued friction and debate; he would have settled
nothing, but only prolonged the furor. As it was, he poured
oil on the troubled waters and buried forever a most em-
barrassing question. Later councils, religious and secular,
would have done more for the race had they done that. For
by compromise we get things done; by compromise we estab-
lish at least a minimum of understanding, and with it clear
the road. The Jerusalem Council realized that; they knew
in their hearts that they were met, at last, for one great purpose: to clear the road, to reunite the Church, to make it
strong and not divided to carry on. To their everlasting
honor, the elders and Apostles did just that. They settled in
a fine high mood of Christian charity the most awkward
dilemma ever to face the faith. They prevented a schism, a
division. They averted a split and a disaster that would have
wrecked everything.

Paul and Barnabas hurried back to Antioch, accompanied
by two new missionaries, Judas Bar-Sabas and Silas. Antioch
read the news in their sparkling eyes, before they spoke a

word. Antioch listened closely as the letter from the Council was read to them, at a mass meeting. The letter began: "The Apostles and [the] elders and brethren send greeting unto the brethren which are of the Gentiles in Antioch . . ."! Brethren! They were that now, without proviso, without a qualification. The gate had been thrown open; they came through it cheering as the reader read on. Abstain from idolatry and sacrificial meats? They would gladly. From blood? They were ready for that; there was but one blood of interest to them now, the blood of Christ. Fornication? That was gone out of them before the letter arrived; their old rituals were dying of their own shame. They wept and laughed and sang and prayed; they turned their mass meeting into a prayer meeting.

The four tarried a while in Antioch, to catch their breath and heal the Church and to consider the road. They saw the road open, clear of fences, devoid of the old stumbling-blocks; they were as runners on their marks, impatient for the signal to be off. One morning Antioch awoke to find Judas gone, gone they knew not where, just gone out on the road. Another day, and Barnabas had sailed away for Cyprus, with young John Mark. The last to go were Paul and Silas, who went together, off across Asia, looking for the road to Europe.

Paul was free: he had been let loose upon the world. Undisputed was the title he had earned and claimed: Apostle to the Gentiles. No man, no sect, no tradition ever challenged that again. From the moment he had heard James read his great decision, Paul knew his work was clear. He was to range the world with his Lord. He was to make Christ the hope of Everyman. He did it. In three long journeys he covered the Greek world; he preached in the metropolis and the back-country town; he and his Christ came to be familiar travelers from east to west and back again. He was a man without a country, a man of all countries, a citizen of the world; his far-visioned eye held in proper focus every land and clime from Rome, the center of the world, to Spain, the end of it. His spirit took in all, and knew no border; he dreamed of a new world order. His great soul recognized no man as slave, or master, or Greek or Jew or Roman; he recognized no circumcision or uncircumcision, no barbarian, Scythian, bond nor free; he knew only *men,* men made one in Christ. He made men see that, think that of one another; he lifted men from the slime of the commonplace and pointed them to the stars.

He lifted Christianity from the status of a minor sect and made it a world religion; he swept over and through and beyond the old religions, gave them a consummation in Christianity, cleared the air and recharged the atmosphere like a sudden sanctified hailstorm. He gave the new faith a theological box in which to preserve its truth; he wrote one quarter of the New Testament and he inspired Doctor Luke to write another quarter. He wrote Galatians, and when Martin Luther read Galatians, the Reformation was begun. He succeeded by carrying the world in his heart, where Atlas had failed to carry it on his shoulders. He worked out the daydream of Archimedes: he thrust the lever of a great faith beneath the world, and he moved it.

The Council of Jerusalem! Without it and its judgment, the Tarsan could never have done what he did. James the Just! Did he know how just he was? Paul, Apostle to the Gentiles! One of the church fathers describes him aptly: "Three cubits in stature, he touched the sky!" That tells it all. Without him, without this "man small in size, with meet-

ing eyebrows, with a rather large nose, baldheaded . . . "
without him, which way would we have turned in 50 A.D.?
What travail and defeat should we have met along the road,
and at what fearful destination should we have eventually
arrived?

III

CONSTANTINE
AND THE EDICT OF MILAN

GATHERED on a plain in Bithynia were the marching men of
Rome, their helmets and their armor bright as silver in the
sun, their high-flown battle banners exulting in the soft Asian
wind. Murmurings of soldier-gossip rippled through their
ranks; they talked in solemn, studied monotones to one
another. An incredulous thing was about to happen, a most
remarkable and unbelievable and inexplicable thing. A great
king was about to give away his scepter and his throne. An
emperor was abdicating, of his own free will.

In all the iron record of the Empire, this thing had never
come about before. Once a king, always a king; they died
in harness, in the purple. But this Emperor, this Diocletian,
only fifty-nine and at the zenith of his glory, was quitting,
resigning, going away. Twenty years an emperor, he'd had
enough of it; for twenty years he'd promised to do it, looked
forward to it, after uniting the Empire. The day had arrived;
he was turning his back on the turmoil of politics and the
hazards of war to live out what was left for him in the peace
and quiet of the farm. He was going out to Salona, to raise
cabbages and grow old gracefully and to die in bed. And he
was leaving them, his legions, his Empire.

The legions were more interested in the Empire than they
were in his cabbages. Who would get it? Who would be
Emperor? Who would command the armies? They were

[40]

blood-brothers assembled to hear the reading of a will, spoils-men come to see the spoils divided. Who . . . ? He did not leave them long in doubt. Standing on a great raised plat-form on a hill in the plain, he threw the Empire down into the hands of four strong men. Galerious and Constantius were to act as emperors; Maximin Daza and Severus were to command the troops. The Abdicator rode off happily, to his cabbage-patch; the soldiers turned back to their tents, still muttering. Some liked it. Some didn't.

In the little group of favored ones about Diocletian stood a trim young human god with ears that drank in every word and eyes that saw everything. He belonged there, behind Diocletian; the fates had in him the perfect man-behind-the-throne. Keen mind. Powerful body. Restless and ambitious spirit. This was young Constantine, son of Constantius. Young Flavius Valerius Aurelius Constantinus. His was the majestic head of a prince, set on a soldier's shoulders. Hand-some. High-spirited. Thirty-five years old. Born to the purple. Fearless. He towered, even beside the Emperor. An eagle, in the company of sparrows. Diocletian had sensed the power that rippled in that supple body and in that strong mind; he watched the natural grace and charm with which this Prince moved about on the battlefield and in the court, and he promoted him, quickly, over the heads of the less promising. The generals sensed his power and his future too; they knew his every move. He knew theirs. Tiger watching tiger. Lion stalking lion. Some day . . .

The young Prince accepted Diocletian's cutting of the pie of Empire without a word; he returned to his soldier duties, said nothing, watched everything. He knew what would happen; there was not room in Rome or in all this Roman Empire for two emperors, to say nothing of four. The vultures would fight, exhaust, and kill one another; they were pirates brawling over treasure-chests on the deck of a sinking ship. Whoever was strongest would survive; the fittest, the cleverest would emerge from the mêlée with the reins in his hands. And Constantine, aware of the strength of his own right arm, meant to gather in those reins.

The hour struck within a year; in 306, Constantius died in Britain, with his last breath commending his son to the favor of his troops. The father was not yet in his grave when the troops replied; they lifted their broadswords with a shout in the air, and called him Emperor Constantine! The young man smiled, returned the salute, and notified all other pretenders to the throne that now they could reckon with him. By 308, the number of "Emperors" had increased to six. By 310, thanks to the unnatural selection of murder, suicide and defeat in battle, there were but three: Licinius watched the East, Maxentius was guarding the Tiber and Constantine was keeping a watch on the Rhine, in Gaul. These three might have drawn a pact, divided their realms, and ruled in peace. They didn't. They were ambitious. Most ambitious of the three was Constantine, who took his time and took no chances and made no mistakes.

There was peace of a sort between them until 312, peace that was too good to last. At least two of them were driven by one common, insatiable ambition: Maxentius and Constantine wanted to rule, alone, to restore what Diocletian had built, a united Empire. Maxentius broke the spell: he moved first; he said the provinces of Gaul, where Constantine watched and waited, were really his, and he meant to have them. He sounded his trumpets, mustered his troops, and started down the road for Gaul. He had not marched a mile when Constantine, informed of it, struck his tents and hurried his army down the Rhine, on the double-quick. He took that army across the Alps, à la Hannibal, fell on an amazed Maxentius in northern Italy, sent him reeling back in panic and disorder to the very gates of Rome. Nine miles from Rome, Constantine called a halt, to rest his men, bury his dead, lay out his battle. From the hills around Rome his men, eager for the kill, looked down upon their prey. The men of Maxentius swarmed on the walls. The world stopped. Time stood still. Tomorrow, the blow would fall. When these two armies clashed, one age would die and another would begin. It was the breaking-point between ancient history and the Middle Ages.

Behind the walls, the pagan citizens of Rome idly tossed their pinches of incense on the altars of their many gods and vacantly prayed that Constantine might win. They had had enough of Maxentius; he was a brute, a tyrant, a coward and a lout. The Christian citizens of Rome sent forth their prayers to their one God, sans incense; they may have prayed for either war-lord, or for either army, or for neither. They had little to gain and little to lose, whoever won. They were a niggling minority; they were at best one-twelfth of the Empire's population. For three hundred years they had either been laughed at or persecuted; they had almost as many dead martyrs as living members. Nobody heard their prayers. Nobody listened, except themselves and their one God.

Meanwhile, strange doings were afoot in the camp of Constantine. Plans were becoming involved with praying, superstition with strategy. Always, before a battle, the Romans sought the help of the gods; of *one* of the gods, the one god whose favor would surely lead them to victory. Whoever, they said, was skillful in attracting the divine assistance of the proper diety would triumph. Castor and Pollux, they knew, had helped them hurl back Hannibal; Julius was lucky enough to enlist the aid of Venus Genetrix at the battle of Pharsalus, and Julius had won; Augustus had put his trust in Apollo at Philippi and Actium, and Augustus had won! Problem to be solved by Constantine: which god should *he* choose? He was a tolerant man, this Constantine, so far as the gods were concerned; one man's altar was as good as another, to him, and he had never interfered with any man's prayers, anywhere. But now there was a battle to be won; now the correct god must be placated. Which one? All the gods in the polytheistic gallery of Rome, at one time or another, had failed one or another of his predecessors. Which god now? He was worried about it. He tossed in his sleep. He had a dream, we are told. And a vision.

This is trembling ground for the historian; whoever tries to tell or write of the vision or the dream must needs move warily, for he has but two sources of information, and both of them are sinking sand. His sources are Eusebius, Bishop of Cæsarea, close friend and uncompromising champion of Constantine, and Lactantius, an amiable African who wrote lurid and breathless history but not always accurate history. Both let their hearts run wild with their heads; both reveled in superlatives in describing their hero; both are, therefore, suspect. Lactantius tells us that in a dream Constantine was told (by Christ, who came and stood at his bedside) to place on the shields of his soldiers the divine sign of the cross. He says nothing of any vision. Eusebius adds that, years later, telling us that after the dream came the vision of the cross in the clouds, above the army of Constantine, and with the cross the words, "Conquer by this."

Whatever the truth or nature of the vision and the dream,

[44]

this happened: the soldiers of Constantine drew up for battle with the monogram of Christ upon their shields. Above their heads floated a new standard, the Labarum; in place of the screaming Roman eagle, on that standard, were the initials and the cross of Jesus Christ. Constantine had forsaken Apollo for Christ! Why not? Had not the Christians told him that this was the one God above all gods?

In the cool of the morning, the gates of Rome swung wide and out came the army of Maxentius, to give battle in the open. They crossed the Tiber and stood with their backs to it; their single avenue of retreat, in case of defeat, was the little Milvian Bridge. Right there Maxentius defeated himself; no general worthy of the name ever fights with his back to water, with a flimsy bridge as his only way out in event of rout. None but a fool could have taken such a position. Maxentius took it; down upon him came the roaring legions from the hills. Yards in front rode Constantine himself, charging at the head of his Gallic horse. The earth shook with the impact as horse crashed down upon man. There was no stopping this. Maxentius' men stood for a moment, wavered, cracked, broke, turned in headlong panic for the bridge, the hoofs of frenzied horses and the swords of Constantine at their backs, crowding them, crushing them, cutting them down, jamming them together helplessly into the ghastly bottle-neck of the bridge. Scores fell, unable to lift their swords to fight back; whole companies were pushed from the banks and from the bridge into the swirling waters, dragged down by the weight of their armor, drowned.

That afternoon, a squad of Constantine's men waded into the Tiber and dug the body of Maxentius from the mud. They dug long, and very deep. It was just fifty-eight days since they had left the Rhine.

Constantine called his finest chariot and went in through the gates of the City of the Seven Hills, master of the West. (Licinius was safely pocketed, in the East.) Ruler now, with the emblem of the Christ upon his banners. A conqueror hailed by a fickle city quite used to hailing. Rome went mad. Rome cheered him, and the bronzed veterans behind him. Rome stared at the new Labarum, at the cross on the spearhead. Rome jeered, like coyotes jeering a dead hunter, at the sight of the grisly head of Maxentius carried on another spear, among the Labarums. The bloody head of the fallen foe, and the cross of the Prince of Peace! Rome's Christians stood on the curbstones, speechless, bewildered, wondering.

Constantine hated Rome; he stayed there only two months, just long enough to arrest and kill every last one of the family of Maxentius, to set up for himself a statue in gold, making himself look like a god in gold, holding in his hand a spear shaped like a cross. Rome built for him a grotesque triumphal arch, the "Arch of Constantine," decorating it with marbles and sculpture stripped from the arch of Titus. (Titus was dead!) On one side of the arch they carved the words, "To the Liberator of the City"; on the other, "To the Founder of Our Repose." The Christians might well have carved the latter legend above their temple doors, for in it there was a sweet poison, a subtle irony to be worked out by subtle time. Constantine, thanking their God for his victory, became at once their liberator and the founder of their repose.

The conqueror thanked Rome for the statue and the arch, and hurried off to Milan. At Milan he gave the hand of his sister to Licinius in marriage. (Later, he had Licinius executed.) And at Milan, with Licinius, he put his hand and signature to one of the most significant documents in the history of this world. We call it the Edict of Milan. It is the first Magna Charta, expressing the gratitude of a great Roman and the tolerance of a great spirit. In part it reads:

"We (Licinius and Constantine) have decided . . . to grant both to Christians and to all others perfect freedom to practice the religion which each has thought best for himself, that so whatever Divinity resides in heaven may be placated, and rendered propitious to us and to all who have been placed under our authority. . . . Henceforth, in perfect and absolute freedom, each and every person who chooses to belong to and practice the Christian religion shall be at liberty to do so without let or hindrance in any shape or form."

Free! The Christians rubbed their eyes, like prisoners let out into the light. After three hundred years of uncertainty and terror and persecution, they were free to come up out of their caves and their catacombs and set up their altars where they chose, to worship God in the sunlight, in the Forum, in the street. They could build their churches above-ground, meet and pray and read their scriptures without fear of arrest or pagan gibe. They could accept public office; their clergy would rank with the priests of Apollo and Venus Genetrix; their ecclesiastical courts would be recognized. At the stroke of a pen, or a quill, they were lifted from ridicule to respectability. The Kingdom of God had come!

They were lifted to even more than tolerance and respect; at the noble gesture of most noble Constantine they were lifted high in royal favor, above all other sects in Rome. He gave them not only recognition, but the power and the disposition to rule: he thrust the scepter of the Cæsars into their hands. He brushed from their skirts the dust of the catacombs and dropped on their astounded and delighted shoulders the royal purple of the Emperors. What else could he have done? Had not their Christ strengthened him against Maxentius, given him the victory? He was not one to forget this; with this God he had conquered, and to this God he would render what was justly due. He outdid himself in the rendering. He spilled upon the Church great sums of silver and of gold from the imperial treasury; he gave the Church land by the acre, by the mile; he made light the burden of taxes. He exempted their ministers from civil obligations, he made them in time a privileged class. And as his largess and his admiration for the Church increased, he took temples and land from the pagan congregations and gave them to the Christians. He built churches himself; magnificent, priceless structures, in the East and in the West. He piled gift on gift, privilege on privilege. All he asked in return was the continued favor of the Christian God, the soothing, unifying application of the Church's faith and spirit and teaching and organization upon the State, to give the State that sense of unity and order which was so sadly lacking.

Is this harsh judgment? Unfair to Constantine? Read the Edict again. He set free every Roman to practice in perfect freedom his own religion, *"that so whatever Divinity resides in heaven may be placated, and rendered propitious to us . . ."* There is a mirror to Constantine's mind, revealing his motives. *All* the gods are recognized here, that *whatever Deity* . . . He had done it before, years before, when he signed the same sort of edict with Galerius, closing it with a plea for the Christians to remember the Emperor in their prayers! Whatever Deity reigned, that Deity Constantine wanted on his side; he would protect and prosper the Church of that Deity to keep it on his side. Perhaps his attitude may be better mirrored in a story told of Helena, his mother.

Helena made a pilgrimage to the Holy Land, and brought back to Constantine two true nails from the true cross. Constantine had them hammered into a bit for the mouth of his horse. It is quite possible, in the light of what we know of the rest of Constantine's life. This Cæsar was ambitious; power was his dominant passion. And while he never utilized the Church, directly, as an instrument to further his political ambitions, while he undoubtedly had a genuine belief in its spiritual character, yet, indirectly, he used the Church and used it well. He used it as a bit, as a check-rein in the mouth of the tempestuous Empire he was trying to saddle and ride; the Church to him was a buffer, a shock-absorber, between himself and the discontent of his subjects. If by strengthening this Church and by placating its evidently mighty God he could get unity in the Empire; if he could tap the bottomless reservoir of spiritual strength in the Church and use it to rouse in his people the will to peace and concord . . . well, why not?

No student can doubt his sincerity; no student can help doubting his Christianity. He had no real conversion, no deep conviction of sin; of the inner experiences and meanings of the Christian faith he knew absolutely nothing. If he did, it was never apparent in his rule across the years that followed Milvian Bridge; in these years he murdered or caused to be murdered Licinius, his brother-in-law; Fausta, his wife; and Crispus, his own son. For the first ten years of his reign, says Aurelius Victor, he was a good ruler; for the next ten he was a robber and for the last ten he was a spendthrift. He waited until death was upon him before he accepted baptism; baptized then, he had little chance of sinning, and he could approach the gates of Heaven with all other sins washed away!

Coolly, knowing perfectly what he was doing, he set about establishing and maintaining order in the Church, that he might have order in the State. Blindly, delightedly, the Church walked into the unintentional trap. Deeper and deeper she sank into the smothering folds of the purple; from her slowly went her freedom and her ancient glory. Into her arms came trooping a multitude who were to do her no good, a multitude of men of wealth and position and less than nominal faith in all the Church had stood for, suffered for. Eating at the royal table in the palace were her bishops and her teachers; at the head of the table sat the Emperor. He kept his eye on all of them, steered their conversation, settled their arguments. He called in the bishops and appointed them to seats of power in the government; he loaded down the clergy with yet more privileges which resulted in centuries of controversy after he was dead and gone. He called their first Councils (and his successors called the rest) and he told the Councils what they could do, and not do. He called a Council at Arles to settle a dispute over the bishopric of Carthage; he, himself, handed down the final decision, enforced it with threat of the royal arms, took from the losers their property, gave it to the winners. He called a Council at Nicæa when Arius and Alexander fell to quarreling over the divinity of Christ, presided over it, umpired it from his seat in a golden chair, called it frankly a silly tempest in the theologian's teapot, an "insignificant subject of controversy" (he had not the least idea what they were talking about), sat helpless and mystified at their involved discussions. But when time came for the decision, he took care of it. He decided against Arius, and enforced his decision on pain of banishment and death. He wrote the rulings of the Councils into Roman law. And heaven help the man who disobeyed that law.

CONSTANTINE AND THE EDICT OF MILAN

Can you see what was happening? Do you see what Constantine, wittingly or no, was doing to the Church, and through the Church to the Middle Ages and to us? Here was the ink still wet on the Edict of Milan, and the specter of intolerance, the old enemy of the Church of Christ, was already back and busily at work. Only now positions were reversed. Now the Church, strengthened with respectability and privilege and power, was demanding of her former persecutors that *they* throw their pinches of incense on the altars of Christ; now the pagans were heretics. When Licinius championed paganism and opposed Christianity, it was the signal and the excuse for Constantine to put him out of the way. When the Donatists lost at Arles, it was the signal for their persecution. When the Arians convinced the Emperor that he had erred at Nicæa, he returned them to power over the Alexandrians; they used their power pitilessly; they persuaded women to baptism by flogging them, even by torture. It was no long step from that to the spectacle of armies marching in the name of God from the African desert to the Black Sea, razing, burning, looting. It is no long step from Constantine pursuing his heretics to the torture-chambers of the Inquisition; no long step from the first appearance of the Labarum to the proclamation of countless holy wars; no long step from the dream of Constantine, with the heavenly messenger telling him to put the Christian monogram on his shields, to that dream of Charles Martel, in which St. Peter told The Hammer to go forth and slay the Lombards; no long step from all this to monks touring Europe, preaching the Crusades; no long step from the cross in armed triumph at the Milvian Bridge to the "white Christ" of the Allied doughboy at Mons and the *"Gott mit uns"* of the German Christian in northern France.

In other words, the policy of Constantine toward heresy and

[51]

unity fastened on the Church a spirit of intolerance for sixteen hundred years. It was not Constantine who had captured the Church; he never meant to do that. It was the Church that had surrendered to Constantine. The Church stepped up willingly into the chariot of State, made of it the vehicle on which it rode to power. For a while, Cæsar drove, and the Church was a happy and contented passenger; but Cæsar's grip slackened as the Empire weakened, and when the barbarians swarmed across the road, the Church took over the reins. A Roman Church, borrowing the trappings and the structure and the methods of the State, supplanted the Roman secular power, grasped the falling scepter and ruled for sixteen centuries. And at the end of these sixteen hundred years, another Edict had to come, another fight for freedom had to be made. The Edict was in the form of ninety-five theses tacked on a chapel door in German Wittenberg; the Liberator was Luther, standing against a later Rome, making all over again a stand for tolerance and the right of every man to worship God "without let or hindrance in any shape or form."

Constantine died in the East, in 337; he drew his last breath in his palace in the suburbs of Nicomedia, a stone's-throw from the spot where he had heard Diocletian read his will. His body was placed in a golden bed, says Gibbon, and for days the officers and the courtiers of the Empire knelt uncovered at his silent side, awaiting his command. Constantine was dead; long live Constantine. Long he has lived; he is alive today. The iron ghost of this ambitious Cæsar still pounds his way across our world, still strives to keep his hold upon the Church, to keep it orderly, subservient, to use it as a shock-absorber between himself and the people, a source of holy sanction for his wars, to keep it an uncomplaining passenger in his chariot. In Russia such a subservient Church has been ground to nothing beneath his iron heel. In Germany, a State Church struggles for her life. In every nation of this world, in greater or lesser degree, that' is going on; the chariot rocks as it careens down history's boulevard, rocks as the Church, aware at last of the design of Cæsar, struggles to free itself.

What thinks Constantine, as he watches from his Cæsar's Valhalla? And what think those churchmen of his who sought to give us power to build the Kingdom quickly, but who innocently put in our blood a poison that has deferred its coming these many centuries?

IV

AUGUSTINE AND *THE CITY OF GOD*

ON THE night of August twenty-fourth, the Mistress of the
World lay locked in her death-sleep. She did not know that
she was dying; this was a sluggish slumber, the heavy exhaustion of the bacchanalian. Rome's eyes were weighted shut with
gold; her strength was dissipated, burned out of her wolfish
loins in the fires of lust and revel, her sight blinded with blood
and her eardrums broken by the roaring of the crowd in the
Colosseum. Her men of might were dead and buried; her new
"leaders" spent their days fawning before the current Em-
peror-fool. Now her swordsmen rested their swords, watching
the red play of the gladiators. Those who had taken the sword
were about to perish by the sword. Yet they slept this night,
secure in the fool's confidence that because no enemy had set
his foot in Rome for eight hundred years, no enemy ever could.
Who dared say that Rome could fall? This was the potentate
of earth, the guardian of the world and the world's peace,
builder of cities and highways and waterways and patron of
art and progress and steward of earth's destiny. Fall? Not
Rome. So the Romans slept. And in the shadow of her walls
flickered the campfires of Alaric the Goth, like the gleaming
eyes of wolves in the night.

Rome had been warned: those with ears to hear had long
since caught the echoing of enemy trumpets from afar, coming
nearer, nearer, nearer. Africa was being harried and worried
by constant raids of wild desert tribes; Gaul was overrun by

Franks and Germans; Spain lay in the hand of the Vandal. And arrogant Alaric had been marching, for years, all over Italy, laughing at the papier-mâché opposition of the legions sent out from Rome, mowing them down like hay, slaughtering, burning, helping himself. He had even paid one visit to the Eternal City; the senators had not so long ago bought him off with a king's ransom of gold and silver and scarlet silken cloth and three thousand pounds of pepper. That should have been a lesson. It wasn't. When Alaric had left them with their lives, they laughed at him for being so easily, so cleverly, bought off. They added insult to ridicule and Alaric, enraged, wheeled his battalions and came back. On this night of the twenty-fourth of August, in the year 410, he sat in his tent a mile or so from the treasure-vaults of Capitoline Hill and the Vatican. This time, he vowed, Rome would pay, and Rome would not laugh. The armor of the Roman guards upon the walls caught the glint of the stars, moved about like tiny torches in the dark, like moving fingers, beckoning fingers.

At the stroke of midnight a great lock creaked and the Salarian Gate slid open to a tiny crack, and there were whisperings between a Roman and a Goth. Behind the Roman, within the gate, stood a shadowy handful of legionnaires, a chosen few in on the secret of betrayal; at the Goth's back, pressing into the protecting shadow of the wall, crouched a company of his barbarians, hands clammy on their sword-hilts, eyes fastened on the widening crack. The bargain was driven, the Judas' gold paid; the gate fell fully open as a Gothic trumpet split the silence in a blast at once terrible and triumphant, and the men of Alaric, sleeping on their swords, arose with a shout and poured through the traitor's gate. There was a swift overpowering of the guards, a rush of the barbarian horde down the streets of dreaming, drunken Rome. Before

the first scream had been lifted and stilled in the black canyon
of the night, a Gothic commander stood flat-footed at the heart
of Rome, a terrifying colossus, sword in one hand and torch in
the other, master of a fallen city of the Cæsars not even aware
of his presence, bellowing orders to the savage mob that swept
toward him from every avenue. In the mind of every man of
them was one single, burning thought: loot! The first torch
was touched to the first house, and the Mistress rubbed her
eyes and hastened down to die in the streets of The-City-That-
Could-Not-Fall.

Not many died; some thousands perhaps, but on the whole
not many. The forty thousand slaves who had deserted to
Alaric had their hour; they fell upon their former Roman
masters in a vengeful fury that only exhaustion could check.
Some of the Huns in the Gothic army went the limit. Alaric
did his best to check them, and partly succeeded; he checked
his Goths with a single word. What he wanted was not blood
but treasure, not a city wiped out but a city punished. That
was unique among conquerors. Compared with the Romans
who leveled Carthage with the ground, Alaric was a saint in
armor; compared with Charles V and Spanish Duke of
Alva and many another Christian victor, he was an angel of
mercy. As a matter of fact, Alaric was a Christian; he and
his men were Arians; he was a "barbarian" only insofar as he
was not a Roman. There was something good in the Goth.

He specialized in gold and gems and silk and pepper; this
was a sack, and not a slaughter. He piled his wagons high with
costly plate and vase and whole wardrobes of cloths. What he
couldn't carry, he smashed; priceless statues and marbles were
shattered into bits with the battle-ax. He killed those who
resisted and tortured those who tried to hide their treasure,
sometimes tortured them to death. He burned only a part of

Rome. There he stopped. He gave orders that there was to be no wholesale, needless killing or conflagration. He insisted upon one order above all others: the churches of the city were not to be sacked, nor even entered; their sacred treasures were not to be touched, and all men and women within their walls were to be given sanctuary, immunity from the sword and rack. Sacred vessels and relics were transferred from the smaller churches to St. Peter's; a procession of Goths marched from the Quirinal Hill to the Vatican, bearing on their heads and shoulders a fortune in ecclesiastical treasure, guarded by other Goths and cheered by Romans along the way. And in every church in Rome, the victors found quaking Romans crowded about the altars they had formerly neglected or despised. Any port in a storm. Anywhere to save their lives. Like rats scampering from a foundering ship, they turned from Mars and the sword that had failed them and came wailing back to Christ and the cross.

On the sixth day Alaric left them to their ashes, bearing away their ransom and a column of slaves. He took all he could take, and left Rome broken, left a smoking, pauperized city completely shattered in wealth, health and spirit. Rome might rebuild her palaces and boulevards (which indeed she did, within seven years), but Rome would never threaten him nor any other man again. Break a man's spirit and you have finished him; you may put ermine on him, thrust a title and mace upon him, but he is still refuse on the scrapheap. Rome, her spirit broken, was . . . refuse. Her majesty had wilted, her grandeur perished. The Goth left her a cripple in a world full of war, as thoroughly destroyed as Carthage had ever been. More so, for she was fair prey now for every barbarian horde that came against her; she was to die not once but many times. Some few of her citizens remained to rebuild their wasted fortunes and their looted palaces; most of them, who sought to escape slavery under Alaric or were too lazy to rebuild, scattered like chaff before the wind, north, east, south and west. They wailed their way along the coasts of Syria and Egypt; they rode their wagons of woe across Italy and deep into Asia. They staggered into Constantinople and Jerusalem. They went begging pity and shelter of all the peoples of the earth, of all they had once conquered and denied pity or quarter. A ragged army of them came to Bethlehem, where lived the gentle Saint Jerome, one of the four doctors of the Latin Church and one of the few real lovers of mankind. Jerome broke into tears as he looked upon this deluge of the disconsolate pouring into the town where had been born that Christ who died with a Roman spearwound in His side; when they told him what had happened, he dipped his quill in his tears and wrote:

> "Who would believe that Rome . . . would fall to the ground? that the mother herself would become the tomb of her peoples? . . . that today holy Bethlehem should shelter men and women of noble birth, who once abounded in wealth and are now beggars?"

Jerome put in writing what the whole West was thinking: when Rome fell all fell; the universe had perished in the ruin of one city, for Rome had been the head, the brains, the heart, the nerve-center and the blood-font of the world. All was lost with her. Alaric had snuffed out the candle of man's hope and destroyed the wagon-trains of the march of progress. Mankind had entered the valley of the shadow of death, where all who entered left hope behind. So said Jerome. So thought the world, or most of it.

The West did more than think that; Roman, pagan, Christians half-hearted and anti-Christians blamed it all on God and Christianity. Where had this God been, while all this was happening? Right at the moment of the Christian triumph in Rome, the holocaust had come; indeed, *because* of it, the blow had fallen. Had Rome stood fast by her other gods, this would not have come! Beside themselves with grief and fear and sense of lost estate, the Roman world turned to snarl at God and make Him their scapegoat of misfortune. (A habit still somewhat prevalent!) God and the Church had few defenders and an army of snarlers and critics; this was the ebb-tide of the early Church.

Right at that moment there rose a man, a great lover of God and son of the Church, who listened to the hubbub and who kept his head. In African Hippo, this man wrote a book to defend this God and steady this Church and to answer the foes of the faith. It was a book made up of twenty-two books; a book that was fifteen years in the writing; a book that will outlast the pyramids. It was a dike thrown up by a master-hand against the rising waters of confusion and despair, a dike to save the day for God and the world for men. A book that was a loom on which were gathered in the broken threads of the lost ages. The shuttle was a scholar's pen. The book was called *The City of God*. Its author was Augustine.

Examine him well, this Augustine writing against the tide, for he personifies the struggle of his fellows and his day for truth and light. But for the grace of the God the world was denying, he would have been one of them. As a youth, he *had* been one of them; he was a rake, a spender, a cynic and a fool; so was Rome. He prayed the prayer that his unhappy fellow-rakes were praying: "Give me chastity, but not yet." Rome prayed, "Give us the succor of the gods, but give us license first." He had been one of a club of wild youth who called themselves "The Wreckers"; Rome was a wrecker too. He took a sneering pride, as a young teacher, in "reproving the saints for thinking what they never thought"; Rome had set the fashion for that. He joined first a sect of Manichæans, a mystical, secret sect forbidden by the law (and therefore attractive to youth), who talked in heady wiseness of "the Truth, whilst their heart was void of truth," arguing wearily of "the struggle between the Kingdom of Light and the Kingdom of Darkness," and seldom getting out of the latter, striving fruitlessly to combine Buddha the Hindu and Mani the Persian and Christ the Jew and getting nowhere. He wandered from Manichæanism to Neoplatonism, and found no more light there. Exhausted in his search, he reclined one day under a fig-tree in a garden of Milan; to him there came the voice of a little child, saying over and over: "Take up and read, take up and read." He heard in it the voice of God, rushed into his house and threw open a volume of the writings of Paul. His finger fell upon a verse that read: "Not in rioting and drunkenness, not in chambering and wantonness, not in strife and envying. But put ye on the Lord Jesus Christ . . ."! Then he knew; then he was delivered, in that garden in Milan, from the blind alleys of philosophy and the pitfalls of compromise. Then he put on Christ, then dropped the raiment of the rake and donned the armor of the Lord. Swiftly he equipped himself to take Christ to the wailing world; in quick leaps he rose from convert to baptized churchman, to presbyter; in two years he was Bishop of Hippo. He was that when the first of the refugees came to Africa; he was leader of the Church in Africa, a man strong because he had fought his way out of weakness and cynicism, a man who had been through all these were going through now, and by reason of that, better equipped than any other man to answer them.

At first he pitied them, as a father pitieth his children; but when they turned on God, he turned on them. He met them on their own ground, argument for argument, reflection for reflection, fact for fact. He attacked their prattle of the gods, their abuse of God. Their gods! They were sorry now that they had left their gods. Why, asked Augustine? What had these gods done for them? Where had they been when the Gauls took Rome in 390 B.C.? They had not helped the Romans then. And where were the gods that day when Mithridates had slaughtered eighty thousand of them in one fight? Where were they during the wars and proscriptions of Marius and Sulla? Where were they at the rout of Crassus? Annihilator of Rome's gods was Augustine in the opening chapters of his *City of God;* he lined them up on their pedestals, jabbed them each to the heart with his quill, let the sawdust out of them. Carthage and Hippo began to laugh. These Romans were fools.

They were worse. They were ingrates; they were spoiled children, crying for the moon; they were improvident idiots, begging cake and fiddling while the world burned. What was their first cry as they came to Carthage, asked Augustine? "Pity us, pity us, pity us. Give us meat and drink and a place to sleep. Above all, give us clowns! Give us pleasure, shows, plays, circuses. That's what we've been used to, and that's what we want. Amuse us. Give us pity, plenty, pleasure." They did not crowd the temples, repentent; they crowded the theaters! They sought not strength to start again; they sought levity and laughter, nectar, song, feasting and the feel of silk. They wanted back the gluttony and the vice that had destroyed them. Their ruinous wars had taught them nothing. (What war has ever taught anyone anything?)

Augustine burned them merrily in his spotlight of sense and

nonsense, and put to them finally one blunt question of crowning embarrassment. What of it if Rome *had* fallen? he asked. What difference did that make? He wasn't so worried over it as they were, as Jerome was; he was more concerned with the city of God than he was with the city of Rome. Empires and cities come and go; they always had, and they always would. That was part of God's plan; the houses and the nations built by men were no more than a means to God's ends; they played their little rôles in the timeless drama as the Master Dramatist directed, and then they took their exits from the stage. Rome was but one act, one phase, one city. It was temporal, transient, material. But there was another city that was not temporal, not made by man's hands, but eternal; not material, but spiritual. In that city God was working out His purpose. And in that city lies the real contribution of Augustine; this conception of the inner City of God was the dike that held the flood.

All of us, said the Bishop of Hippo, are citizens of two worlds, not of one. There is the world or the city of man, represented by the State, built on love of self, and disregard of God; like Rome. Then there is the City of God, represented by the Church, built on the love of God and the disregard of self. We live in both at once, and we owe an allegiance to both. *But we owe our first allegiance to the City of God, to the Church.* Only there do we find that which is final and eternal; therefore the Church must take precedence over all else in life. Seek ye first the kingdom of God; go ye first to church.

This was the thought of the book, the substance of *The City of God*. It was just a book. What good is a book? Nine volumes out of ten are written, read and forgotten; nine writers out of ten sleep in lost graves, as completely ignored as the tomes they labored on. Not this one, not this book and not this author. No book has ever meant more to man, no writer ever wrought to finer victory. What Augustine really wrote here was our emancipation from the slavery of uncertainty to the freedom of assurance and faith in the comradeship of God in His Church. Monsieur Poujoulat calls this book "the encyclopædia of the Fifth Century"; it was all of that and more. Not only did it sum up the knowledge of this fifth and previous centuries; not only did it serve as a watershed in which Augustine collected the tides and currents of the thought and culture and faith of the past to send them down, strained and purified, across the Middle Ages; not only was it all of this, but something else. His book was more of a life-boat than a storehouse; it was a modernized Noah's Ark, catching man up from the rising flood and furnishing the vehicle on which he rode out the storm. It gave the Romans the idea of a developing Christendom that was to supplant their fallen Rome. Augustine scraped away the ashes of the ruin of that dead political power, and disclosed the firm, four-square foundation-lines of a new world-order; where Cæsar's throne had stood, he placed the chair of Christ's Vicar, the head of the visible Church.

The shadow of that book fell far across the Middle Ages, deep into the modern era. It made the Church the goal of medieval history; it put the Church above and beyond the reach of the State, gave to the popes their apology and authority to claim power over kings and princes. It inaugurated a struggle between the Holy Father at Rome and the kings of half the earth; it was a declaration of war between powers sacred and secular. It guided the hand of Pope Leo III when he placed the crown on the brow of Charlemagne; Leo's was the hand that rocked the cradle in which lay the infant Holy Roman Empire. With it started monasticism, that trek of the monks away from the cities of men to obscure contemplation of the city of God. With it came the ideal of a Christian Society, of which we hear much today.

He enlarged on the book as the years flew by; he built upon it, and upon his years of study, a system of religious thought which made theology the Queen of the Sciences. Some say this was a rediscovery of Paul's theology; at least it was the first elaborate and comprehensive doctrinal system of the Christian Church. He developed in it his theories of redemption and the Trinity, the sacraments, the freedom of the will; he enlarged upon his theory of the position of the Church. He led the Middle Ages to think of the Church as God's appointed instrument in His effort to save the world, and of the leader of the Church (the Pope) as Christ's personally appointed representative. Here, in this Church, was the bread broken, the body and the blood placed within man's reach; here was the passion and the death of Christ daily re-enacted in the Mass. In the Church's sacraments man found salvation, or he found it not at all. Oh, yes, there were tares in the Church as well as wheat, good men and bad, saved and unsaved, as in the world outside. But that was none of man's business; all man was expected to do was to attend Mass and honor the sacraments and obey the dictates of Holy Church and leave the rest to God, in whose mighty hand was the final threshing of tares from wheat, of saved from lost, of sheep from goats. Honor the Church, respect it, love it, bow to it, for it is of God. Millions still hold that conception; millions of Roman Catholics, passing their church, touch their hats. The Church is the biggest thing in their lives.

And Augustine enlarged upon his theory of grace. Grace, he said, was the free gift of God, and it was irresistible. It was *given* to man; he couldn't earn it. The Father gave it, or the Father withheld; some had it, and some did not. That was predestination, election. Now take up your Calvin, and read what that Reformer had to say of predestination and election. You'll think you're reading Augustine, for in his fifth-century theology are the roots of Calvinism, the head-waters of that river of modified Protestant belief which by now has found its way down from Geneva to every corner of the earth.

Now take up your Luther. Here you read of salvation through grace, and grace alone. Here you read that grace is the free gift of God; here you read that no man can be saved by good works or merit alone. Here is *justification by faith,* the rallying-cry of the Reformation and the bed-rock of Protestantism. Is this Luther speaking, or is it Augustine? It is both.

Now read the record of the controversies between Luther and Calvin and the rest of the Reformers, and you will find them matching the arguments of Augustine against each other. You will discover Luther matching Augustine's doctrine of justification against Calvin with his Augustinian theory of predestination. Read of the arguments of the Reformers against the Catholics, and you watch the play of Augustine's theory of grace, in the hands of the Protestants, against his theory of the supremacy of the Church, in the hands of the Roman. All, all of them, Romans and Protestants and Calvinists and Lutherans and Zwinglians, lean heavily on the Bishop of Hippo. When they were done arguing, they found that this Reformation was no more than the triumph of Augustine's idea of grace over his idea of the Church.

There are those who feel that Augustine brought about as much evil as good, as much struggle as peace; they point to the long and bitter rule of the Middle-Ages Church, with all its holy war and lust for temporal power, its many inquisitions and reigns of terror, its excommunications and indulgences. There is no denying it; such a Church arose, and its leaders claimed Augustine as father and apologist. But those who see that Church and nothing more have something in their eyes, some small mote that hides the beam; they forget that at the heart of this Church, unattractive as it was, were the conquering truths that enabled her to face the world and overcome it. Had there been no such Church, no such strong City of God, well . . . what then? At its worst it was better than anarchy; its feeblest light was a torch in that medieval darkness, a torch that turned the march of man from a road which would have led to certain chaos and ruin, to a road that was man's only escape from the falling walls of Rome. That there were cruel banks of drifting fog and dark along that road we know; but compared with what it might have been, it was the road to Heaven and away from hell. When we followed the summons of Augustine to walk upon it, we escaped Dante's tour of the Inferno and moved toward Paradise. We may be still far from the gate of that Paradise, from that City of God, but thanks to Augustine we are on our way.

V

THE BATTLE OF TOURS

DEEP in the wilderness of Beer-sheba, a mother and her child were lost; their water-bottle was empty, and their strength was gone. The child stumbled, and the mother dragged him to his feet; he fell, and she gathered him into her arms, where he lay white and still, as one dead. Then she fell, moaning and disheveled, wide-eyed, gibbering; she placed him in the shadow of a rock and crawled away, for she could not bear to see him die. She was Hagar, the cast-off concubine of Father Abraham. The child was Ishmael.

To her then came a messenger from God, pointing out to her a hidden well of cool and bubbling water, telling her to lift the child once more, and go on. God, said the angel, had great plans for her Ishmael; he was to become "a great nation." The water-bottle was quickly filled and pressed to the lips of the dying boy; she forced him to his feet, and they staggered on. Somehow, they got through; somehow, they found shelter and a friend in Egypt. Hagar died in Egypt. Ishmael became a great nation.

The roots of this story you'll find in The Book; the rest of it is a blend of fiction, fancy and folklore. All stories are like that, and all histories; their beginnings are always vague, their known facts few. The genesis of the nation of Ishmael, or of any other nation, is lost in guess-work; no man can put his finger on the first of men, families or nations, as Peary put his finger on the pole. We just don't know. It doesn't matter. We are all here. Our whither is more important than our whence.

Only this can we be sure of: somewhere, color and custom and character began; somewhere, some first man stood up in the flowing tide of human blood, and divided as a rock the stream of color, creed and race. Somehow, there came yellow men to the banks of the Yangtze, brown men to the brown Ganges, Indians along the Red River and white men to the Tiber and the Thames. Such men were Ishmael and Abraham; these were forefathers, procreators, patriarchs. Down from Abraham came the blood of Moses, Jesus and the Jew, and after the Jew, as spiritual descendant, the Christian; through Abraham and his son Isaac ("born through promise") ran this stream from Jerusalem to Rome, out of it grew the grace and freedom of Christianity; these were the "chosen people," the people of Peter and the popes. But from that other outcast son, that Ishmael ("born of the flesh"), came others, opposites; from his loins leaped the Arabian, the people of the desert, a people fleshy and sensuous, with renegade eyes forever seeking spoil, with blood hot as the desert sun coursing in their veins. An outcast people, hating the Jew and spitting at the Christian as they passed him in the street, a wild, resentful, Ishmaelitish people who took long years of vengeance on the chosen ones for the short hours of suffering of Hagar and her boy. These we have at one time or another called the Saracens, or the Arabs, or the Mohammedans. They are a great and furious nation, whose very name inspires fear and awe and visions of tents on the desert and raiding Bedouins and muezzins on minarets crying, "Allahu Akhbar. . . . There is no God but Allah!"

For ages, generations, years on end they pitched their tents in that waterless land which lies between Syria and Arabia, and that desert, merciless, made them merciless, resourceful, wily, hard. They were outlaws from the first, with their hand against every man and every man's hand against them. They fought to live. Theirs was a forbidden land, protected from the foreigner by burning sands as Moscow was protected against Napoleon by its white desert of snow. They repelled with the sword whatever invader happened to get across the sands; when there was no invader their commonality was lost, and they fought one another. Their forts were their saddles, the earth was their bed, and the sky their roof. They had no taxes and no kings; they were riders, fighters, nomads, crude in worship and adept with their arms; they prayed to the moon and to ten thousand jinns and wooden idols, and they preyed upon whatever caravan dared come near them. They multiplied in sons and wealth as the years wore on, and they built a great city in the desert. It was their Holy City. It was Mecca. Mecca grew to be glorious. Glorious in culture, and Oriental art, and architecture, and much more. Indeed, there were many lovely spots, many Meccas, all over Arabia, in time. And there were spots touched by Christianity, won by Christianity, and by Judaism, and much that is fine in the religion of the Arab of today came from either or both of these faiths.

Yet, for centuries, they were only roving tribes who loved plunder and hated the "infidel" sons of Isaac and Abraham, strong in lust for vengeance, in fetish and in superstition. Strong, but disunited. Each tribe had its leader, or its leaders, but in all their far-flung land they had not one strong enough to bind their scattered bands into one mighty union. Not, that is, until 570 A.D. In that memorable year, the woman Amina brought forth a son who, according to the story-tellers of the East, cried out immediately he was born: "Allah is great! There is no god but Allah, and I am his prophet!" His grandfather came and took him up to the Kaaba (the "holy place," built upon the very spot where Hagar had found the well), held him high in his arms and named him Mohammed, "the Promised One." Great glory and power would come to his people through Mohammed, said the old man; time proved him modest.

The child grew in wisdom and stature and in favor with the Arabs and with Allah; he was moody and introspective, given to long spells of mystic Oriental dream and vision. He became a driver of camels for a wealthy widow; he married the widow, becoming a man of affairs as well as a mystic. Eventually, inclination conquered occupation; Mohammed wearied of cargoes and caravans, and he forsook his camels for a cause. He retired to a cave, where he could dream in peace and search in leisure for the truth of Allah. The cave was in a dreary desert spot, perfect for his mood; it looked out upon a thirsty waste of rock and sand, where no grass nor shade tree nor anything green could long live; his eyes sank deep, his body wasted; trance and ecstasy and vision held him fast and tortured him, like a man stretched on truth's rack. When he finally came out of his retreat, he was more specter than man; he was a Saracenic John the Baptist, announcing a new faith and a new god. His tidings were not so glad as those of Zacharias' son; he announced no loving Father, no Prince of Peace. He cried out loudly against the idol-worship of his people: "Ye rub them with oil and wax, and the flies stick on them" . . . they were dead wood, and no more, and the jinns were quite as useless. In his cave, said the specter, he had found a new god for the Arabians, the one true god, the One Over All. This was Allah, and Mohammed was his prophet. All men now must listen to him, must give up their jinns and their idols, their old ways of prayer and penitence. All must bow to Allah. To Mohammed's Allah.

Submit! Obey! There it is: there is Mohammedanism, in two words. Surrender yourself, and do Allah's will according to Mohammed's command. Woe, woe, woe to you if you don't. "Woe to the backslider and the defamer . . . They shall be hurled into the fire." That was it: fire! There was no peace here, no love; this was a bloody monotheism, preached by a human torch who set the East afire and cut a wide swath with a holy sword. Cried he: "I therefore, the last of the prophets, am sent with the sword! Let the champions of the faith of Islam [Mohammedanism] neither argue nor discuss; but slay all who refuse to obey the law or to pay tribute. Whoever fights for Islam, whether he fall or conquer, will surely receive the reward. The sword is the key to Heaven and hell!" He swept aside as cowardly the slow method of peaceful persuasion. To arms for Allah! Kill for him, despoil for him, and gain for yourself either the spoil of the infidel, or the richer reward of a sensual heaven, a glory-land of milk and honey and maidens beautiful. Preach the gospel of plunder, fight the Holy War. It was sweet music to the Arab. He could understand this, and he could love it. He gave himself to it, threw himself into Mohammed's cause, a fanatic throwing himself into the fire. And unconsciously he allowed himself to be bound, a scattered people, into a nation. He who for centuries had had no capital nor even temple, gained an empire; he who had been scorned and shunned now felt the earth tremble beneath his rancorous feet. He followed blindly this zealot who never reasoned nor explained, but who swept men off their feet. He was called of Allah to great work, and he threw his goods and his life-blood gladly to the task.

They went from conquest unto conquest; by the time death came into Mohammed's tent they had spread their faith across the whole of the Arabian Peninsula; within a generation after his demise they had conquered it with their swords. Then they burst upon the Persian, crying, "Accept the faith of Islam, and thou art safe . . . A people is upon thee loving death as thou lovest life." Persia fell. The tide of white turbans moved along the shores of Galilee, and before them raced the cry, "The Saracens are coming!" The Romans in Syria fled before these new tycoons of terror; fierce Kalid, "the sword of Allah," sat himself down proudly in the deserted tent of the Roman commander. They swept over all of Palestine and Mesopotamia; they marched past the pyramids and humbled old Egypt in the dust. They entered Asia Minor, Africa; "The Saracens are coming." Before the West could catch its breath, they had poured through the Pillars of Hercules and reined up their steeds in the shadow of a rock called Gibraltar. They moved like a plague across Spain; they were by now

> "A countless multitude,
> Syrian, Moor, Saracen, Greek renegade,
> Persian, and Copt, and Tartar, in one band
> Of erring faith conjoined—strong in the youth
> And heat of zeal—a dreadful brotherhood."

And when they had conquered Spain, they climbed the southern slope of the Pyrenees, and looked with feverish eyes down into Gaul, toward fair France. They were in Europe, and the road to Paris and Rome lay unguarded at their feet! It was exactly one hundred years since Mohammed had died; this was 732.

And what was Europe in 732? Europe was one great Colosseum of chaos. Europe was in that era of anarchy which lay between the fall of Rome and the rise of the Holy Roman Empire. Europe lay stricken, like an exhausted, fallen deer, and across its carcass fought new wolves. The Arab in the East easily tore away half the old Empire; the Germanic tribes crossed the Rhine, in small bands of a thousand or so, and established themselves in petty principalities, under petty chieftains who feared and fought one another; in time, these chieftains settled down to farming, became converted to Christianity, lost their ancient ferocity and aggressiveness, and fell with Europe into her Dark Ages just as the Arab came to his Golden Age. Strongest among them were the Franks, and the Franks were a sorry sight. They were the long-haired and degenerate remainders of the once splendid house of Clovis; they were long on laziness and short on intelligence; yet they alone had some semblance of strength. On solemn church occasions, their leaders road in ox-carts to the church, clutching an ox-goad, clutching it childishly, trying to tell themselves they were still kings clutching scepters. So low had the pomp and majesty of Pope and King come down; all was reduced to a few long-haired, sad-faced young men riding in tottering ox-carts, pretending through the last act of the tragedy, waiting stupidly for their world to fall. It was the moment of moments for the Saracen to ride down the reeling West as the huntsman rides down the spent deer; it was his hour of hours in which to change the face of the world.

Stealthily as a boa-constrictor, the Saracen glided down from his mountain lair and began to wind his fatal coils about the scattered towns on the Gallic plain. There were raids; the Arab struck with dismaying suddenness, raping, burning, killing and disappearing down the road in a whirl of dust before resistance could be organized. To the River Loire and across it went the paralyzing cry, "The Saracens are coming." On the very walls of Paris men and women watched the raiders come insolently close, shout their threats and challenges, and whirl away again. The petty chieftains went into councils- of-war, and looked about them for a man to lead.

Out of the mêlée of the unfit, they pounced upon a strong young Frank. Young Charles (he was Karl, to his Germans), son of Pepin. Charles had a warrior's way about him; he had crowned himself with honor in his struggles against the Frisians, Bavarians, Saxons and Thuringians of the North. He was the only one able to hold these savage tribes in check, and he seemed to be the only soldier in Europe with a ghost of a chance to check the Saracen. Charles. Charles Martel, they called him; Martel meant "The Hammer"; he struck like a hammer, hard, fast, ghost-like, Arab-like. Martel, the grandfather of Charlemagne, and the last hope of the West against the thrust of Mohammed!

The Hammer gathered his Franks and his few allies on that great plain between the cities of Tours and Poitiers; he gathered not an army there, but a militia, a motley mob of contentious barbarians gone soft following the plow, afraid of one another, afraid of the Arab. They faced veterans, an unchecked army of religious zealots who had never yet tasted defeat. Leading the Saracenic host was Abderrahman Ibn Abdillah Alghafeki, valorous cavalryman who longed to lay down his life at the Prophet's feet; leading the Christian militia was an obscure guerrilla chief, suspected by the Christians of adherence to the Wodenism of his ancestors.

But who stood at Tours is not so vital as what stood there. Here were two cultures, two languages, two creeds, two civilizations; here Cross and Crescent faced each other, the cause of the Prince of Peace against the cause of the Mohammedan sword. Bible versus Koran. Christianity versus Islam. One or the other must win, must rule the West. On the outcome of this battle hung the fate of all mankind; upon the victory of either despoiler of the dead Roman Empire depended the subsequent course of world civilization.

Near the Loire, the Hammer drew up his men; they were foot-soldiers, infantry, and their long-haired leader told them just to stand, to hold, to die there if need be, but not to break their lines. The Saracen must not pass. Abderrahman mounted his cavalry on fresh steeds, incited them to maniacal fury with a wild and artful harangue on the Prophet and the Prophet's Heaven and the Prophet's cause, and led them down toward the massed battalions of the Franks. The Christians gripped their spears and set their feet more firmly as they heard the battle-cry: "Allahu Akhbar ... Allah! Allah! Allah!" Headlong they came, plunging, savages on horseback, their horses' hoofs raising a deafening thunder and their cavalry sabers flashing, a fascinating avalanche of death. They crossed the plain; with a sickening thud heard miles away, they leaped upon the wall of fair-haired Franks, hacking, stabbing, chopping, screaming. Horseman and foot-soldier were mixed instantly in a deadly, rough and tumble madness; all fought blindly, stabbing in all directions. The dust lifted for a moment, and the shouting met a lull, and the Franks discovered that their line had held! Amazed, the Moslems drew back across the plain, reformed their lines, came on again. Martel rode among his men, closing up his gaps, stationing fresh men in the front line; when the Saracen struck the wall again, he found the Christian standing spreadeagled over his dead and wounded, still immovable. The second charge failed, and the third, and the fourth; the falling of the sun checked the slaughter at last. There were torches on the field that night; the Arab was taking off his dead, envious of their passage to the Prophet's Paradise; the Christian was burying his fallen under the sign of the cross. There were torches on the field for six successive nights!

In the first gray of the dawn of the sixth day, the Moslems tried again. They met a new, enheartened wall of spears; they fought in desperation now, as men with all to gain and naught to lose; they must win now, or hope was gone. They cut a path into the center of the Christian host, and looked behind to find that Martel had cut off their retreat, flanked them, jammed them into a huddled island entirely surrounded by a sea of Frankish swords. They hacked their way out of the iron circle, and raced about the field, decimated, disorganized, falling slowly back before the slow ponderous, steam-roller advance of Martel's men, who now saw victory within their reach. Abderrahman galloped up and down the field, shouting to his men, waving his sword as a rallying-point, but the rout was too complete. There was no rally; the Moslems had had enough. They ran from the field, leaving the gallant commander to be surrounded and pierced with a hundred spears, to be dragged from his saddle and trampled to death. The Franks pressed them close, driving them. As night fell, the rout halted; the last Mohammedan had disappeared, and the foremost of his pursuers dropped, exhausted, in his tracks. The field was literally carpeted with the dead.

Miracle? The hand of Providence? This victory may have been due to that, and to the over-confidence of the Moslem and the desperation of the Christian. Patriotism and religion combined in the Frank to give him power to stand. He stood with his back to the wall, and he knew it. While the Arab wanted more spoil and territory and conversions, the Frank wanted only to hold what he had. It was do or die; it was stop the Moslem or lose all.

And much as we despair of the combination of religion and

the sword, much as we hate war and all its works, we will admit, in light of circumstance, that at Tours the sword saved the cross. The soldiers of the Crescent never crossed the Pyrenees again; they and their faith remained prisoned in the East, with Constantinople as their western outpost. Europe was safe. Disunited, but secure, and forever immune from the threat of the Prophet. Fresh troubles came; this was no war to end war, no blood-red dawning of an age of peace. But left to her own troubles, the West solved them and moved on confidently to her larger destiny. On the tombs of the fallen of Tours are built the governments and nationalities of modern Europe, the culture and the faith and freedom of the West. Abhorrent as some phases of our Western progress may have been, it was progress nevertheless; the West has far outdistanced the stagnant, Islamitic East. So "decisive battle" is faint praise for this struggle of Saracen against the Hammer. Had the Franks broken on that plain, we would have mosques today instead of churches, the Koran instead of the Bible; we would be teaching our children the learning and the lore of the Arabian and not the learning and lore of the Christian. We would be placing our trust in the armed fist, instead of condemning it and searching for a better way; we would be accepting the sword of Mohammed as the key to Heaven and to hell, instead of the spirit of the Prince of Peace. Tours, bloody and barbaric as it was, accomplished that.

VI

THE BATTLE OF WORMS: MARTIN LUTHER

THERE is a tenseness and a turbulence in Wittenberg. The turbulence is laughter, rolling across the university campus in the center of the town, student laughter, the hilarity of boys on a holiday; the tenseness is in the mien and movements of the professors, who stand in groups beneath the campus trees, or sit moodily in their study chairs, like men awaiting the advent of calamity. On an ivy-covered wall there is a notice, an invitation:

> "Let whosoever adheres to the truth of the Gospel be present at nine o'clock at the Church of the Holy Cross outside the walls, where the impious books of papal decrees and scholastic theology will be burnt. . . . Come, pious and zealous youth, to this pious and religious spectacle. . . ."

It is not so pious to the students. This is a day off. But the teachers, whose sharp and mellowed eyes can read between the lines, know they are on the eve, at this moment, of something more fateful than funny. The notice is signed by young Professor Luther, who teaches Bible.

This Professor Luther is a most courageous man. All Wittenberg, all Germany, admires him. Wherever he preaches, the church is crowded; whatever he writes, men read. For these books and sermons are diatribes against the Roman Catholic Church. Scholastic rebel and a monk himself, this is one man against a mighty institution; he has turned words into darts and is shooting them into Rome. The Pope is alarmed at that; he has spoken sharply to the upstart professor, bidding him bow to Rome, giving him a grace of sixty days in which to recant, to take back what he's said, to say he was wrong. And now the professor invites the students and the town to watch him throw the Pope's letter, in which these demands are made, into a bonfire! Holiday, indeed. Other men had acted so against commands from Rome, and those other men were dead.

The crowd gathers early; the townspeople march behind the professors, out to a great field beyond the University walls. They made a singing ring around the blaze; they cease singing as Doctor Luther steps forward and flings into it the Holy Father's letter, with the words: "Since thou hast afflicted the Lord's Holy One, may fire unquenchable afflict and consume thee." The crowd cheers, and sings the *Te Deum*. The teachers take their way pompously back to their ivied halls. The students prance about the fire; they dress up one of their number in the vestments of the Pope, try to throw him into the river and chase him all over town, in mock anger, while shopkeepers put up their blinds against the fun. They know these boys. Doctor Luther knows them, too. Next day in a sermon he warns them that this was no comedy.

That was the college town of Wittenberg, in December of 1520. Three months later, on the twenty-eighth of March, a dense crowd is in Rome. In the square before the Basilica, the Papal guards struggle to hold back an army of pilgrims who have come to receive the benediction of the Pope. Flowers decorate the square; wax candles burn everywhere within the church. Bells boom as the Pope is carried in his chair out on the balcony, brilliant in his robes, the object of all eyes, the most powerful man in the world. He makes the sign of the cross thrice over the kneeling throng, takes up a document, reads. The square is quiet as the catacombs as the fearful words fall:

"To preserve the holy communion of the faithful, we follow the ancient rule, and accordingly do excommunicate and curse, in the name of God Almighty . . . the Cathari . . . the Arnoldists . . . the Wicklifites, the Hussites. . . . and Martin Luther, recently condemned by us for a like heresy, together with all his adherents, and all persons, whosoever they may be, who aid and abet him. . . . In like manner, we excommunicate all pirates and corsairs . . ."

These are terrible words, the words that sever Wyclif, Huss, Luther, pirate and corsair from the protection of the Church and the hope of Heaven. This is the worst that can happen to a man. The Pope reads on, and on, and on; the roll of heresy is long; when he has finished, he tears it into bits and throws it to the crowd. The pilgrims scramble for the pieces; they are holy relics, miraculously potent. The ruler of Christendom is carried indoors; the pilgrims disperse. The Cardinals feast. The poor of Rome munch their dirty crusts in silence, in an awe that gags them.

A bonfire in Germany, and a kneeling multitude in Holy Rome: put the two together and you have a panorama of Europe on the eve of the Protestant Reformation. Awe and rebellion. Men in blinders, and afraid; men restless, pulling at the blinders, infuriated, yet tense and hesitant. On the one hand the Pope, the regal head of an institution that holds tight the check-rein in mankind's mouth, an institution adamant and error-proof, gigantic, irresistible. On the other, an unhappy monk before a fire, burning a Pope's command as the Pope had burned Huss, with quite the same words of condemnation; the glee of those who watch him is pitted against the blind devotion of the throng in the Basilica; it is the glee, the joy of a world that has waited weary years for one to come and set them free from this terrifying power; it is the releasing of long-pent forces about to burst in international conflagration. This Church, corrupt, is a galling yoke across the neck of Europe; the kneeling crowd in Rome is Europe in miniature. By a gesture of his finger, says this Pope, he could lift a serf to the gold-paved streets of Heaven; by the mere word of mouth he could damn a king's soul to everlasting hell. Such power Europe had seldom seen; it took in not only the earth but Heaven as well. Used wisely, nobly, charitably, it might have made earth a better Eden; abused, it would sire fear, rebellion and ruin to itself. Rome, alas, missed her chance, and abused it.

For centuries before the bonfire, Rome had been descending the long stairway from consecration to corruption; mingled with the sweet incense of her altars was the nauseating odor of profanity and desecration. Priests rushed like scoffing jesters through the Mass, the sooner to return to their cups; when humble Brother Martin Luther, as an Augustinian monk, went down to the Holy City in 1510, to say his Masses reverently in the mother Churches of his honored faith, he found Italian clerics prodding his back in rebuke for his slowness, whispering to him, "Hurry up. Hurry up!" They said three Masses while he said one. Some of them were open cynics; even at their altars they changed words, made a comedy of the miracle; they vied in trying to be funny in their sermons, one chirping like a cuckoo, another hissing like a goose. In many sections, priests paid the bishop for the privilege of

[81]

living with women. One bishop, says Erasmus, received such a tax from eleven thousand priests in a single year. Monks ran taverns. There were monkish brawls in bar-rooms. The people knew it, and the people talked.

But this corruption, evil as it was, was not alone responsible for the Reformation; the Church was already being reformed, from within. There were other more dangerous, more infuriating abuses: the love of money, for instance. Rome needed money and Rome collected it, from everyone, for everything. Rome sold civil offices to ambitious civilians; Pope Leo X made five hundred thousand ducats (one hundred and twelve million five hundred thousand dollars) annually from the barter of some two thousand offices. Criminals bought their way clear of the courts; marriage dispensations were sold on a sliding scale, according to ability to pay, sixteen grossi for an ordinary man, twenty for a noble, thirty for a duke. First cousins could marry for twenty-seven grossi, an uncle and a niece for four ducats. There was a notation on the papal books about this: "Note well, that dispensations or graces of this sort are not given to poor people." The poor knew that, all too well. But what could they do about it?

The poor *could* buy indulgences. He who bought an indulgence from the Church simply bought his way out of punishment, here or hereafter, for his sins. There was plenty of sinning, so the indulgence-sellers had a big market. There was a sliding scale here, also: pennies for the petty sins of little men, fortunes from princely thieves and murderers. The public was going bankrupt, trying to keep paid up; the public was growing tired of draining local treasuries for the benefit of an insatiable Rome. Martin Luther was especially tired of it and angry over it, and he said so.

The public was revolting, for the public's eyes were being

opened to a new earth and a new Heaven. There had been a Renaissance, and life was different; that awakening had led men to believe that life was not a dim and dismal journey lighted only by the whimsical lamps of Rome, but a truly glorious journey lighted by the lamps of man's divine creative instinct and his constant struggle for improvement. The world was growing while Rome was standing still. Columbus crossed the ocean in 1492; Vasco de Gama doubled the Cape in '98, and reached India. There were new clocks, glass windows, chimneys, telescopes and microscopes. Gunpowder and new cannons were blowing down the castles of the feudal lords, blowing away an old economic order, announcing a new patriotism, a new contention between papal and secular political interests. John Gutenberg was printing a Bible in Mayence, using strange new printer's type and a printing press; books, after this, were legible, cheap, easy to get; the ancient veil of peasant's ignorance was rent in twain, and John Everyman discovered reading and literature. Popular education was being born, crying lustily; the Universities were progressing from a rich man's privilege to a common right, and they were teaching a new science and learning at which Rome blanched. (Here's food for thought: the Reformations of Wyclif, Huss and Luther were all university-born.) Rome, sitting on the lid of the old world and wanting to stay there, objected to all this; she wanted no change, no new world. She cried to this bursting age not "Forward!" but "Mark time!" She was an old institution in a new universe, and when the flint of her tradition struck the bright steel of progress, there were sparks; sparks that touched off the Wittenberg bonfire.

As Doctor Luther reminded his students the day after the holiday, this thing was serious; it became more so, with every hour. Things went from bad to worse, from fun to fury, from smolder to fire. There were more firm demands from Rome that he change his ways and keep quiet; there were more virulent refusals from him, more tracts, more books. He couldn't retract, he said, for he'd had a vision from God, and one with a true vision from Him never retracts. High in a tower on his campus, Luther had read one day the words of Paul: "The just shall live by faith," and a bright light, a Damascus-road light, had broken over him in a dazzling cloud. By faith were men saved or through lack of it lost; by faith in the atoning work of Jesus called the Christ, and not by whim of Pope or Church's sacrament. By faith, by submission to the will of God as revealed in Holy Scripture and not by submission to the priests, the bishops, the cardinals. The Bible was more important than the Mass. The Church was neither infallible nor indispensable; faith was the key whatever Rome said or did, whatever happened to her, in her, through her. Luther wrote that and preached that and taught that, while Rome listened and went on from mild concern to stern determination to stop him. Such a man was dangerous; such teaching was heresy, a threat to the Church. Stop it, Martin Luther! Submit to Rome. Acknowledge the authority of the Holy Mother Church, or accept the consequences. Learned doctors came down to debate with him, to confound him; he confounded them. They were weak waves lapping at Gibraltar. The fire spread out from Wittenberg, until all Europe was ablaze. And two rulers, Italian Pope and Spanish Emperor Charles V, watched warily this fire, this spreading dissent, this creeping unrest. Unrest in the Church meant unrest in the State. Unity and peace in one meant unity and peace in the other. So it was that Charles V, concerned not so much with religion (of which he knew little) as with holding his grip on the loose confederation of German states, summoned Luther to appear at an Imperial Diet, or court, to be held at the ancient city of Worms. It was an imperial command. Would Luther dare refuse to go, as he had refused the summons of the Pope?

His friends begged him to do just that; they were terrified. Going to Worms was going to certain death; Rome had already pleaded with the Emperor to break his promise of safe-conduct to the rebel, to betray him on the road to the assassins of Rome, who would take care of him. Even if he got to Worms, he would be a lamb in a slaughter-house. One of the Pope's delegates to the Diet was to be Cardinal Aleander, who had once killed five peasants because his pet dog had been somehow killed. Why gamble his life in the hands of such a man? They'd kill him, one way or another. But Luther laughed. To one of his frightened fellow professors he wrote: "Dear Brother, if I do not come back, you go on teaching and standing fast in the truth; if you live, my death will matter little." Such a man was the man Luther.

On the morning of April second, he climbed with three companions into a wagon at his door; it was a wagon donated by the town, filled with straw and covered with a makeshift awning; this was liberty's chariot; this was the world's bravest liberator, riding with a lute in his lap. Before the wagon rode young Caspar Sturm, the Emperor's herald, carrying a great yellow banner with the imperial eagle emblazoned on it, clearing a path for the professor, in the name of His Majesty Charles V. In every town there were cheers and hisses; this was the most hated and beloved man in all Germany, in all the world. Leipzig was cool to him; Naumberg cheered, and one valiant priest thrust a portrait of the martyr Savonarola into the cart, crying to Luther, "Stand fast!" At Erfurt, where he had been a university student, there was a banquet; at Eisenach, where he had been born, he was ill, and a doctor bled him. Veiled threats came to him. Even Caspar Sturm became alarmed and asked him if he really meant to go on; Luther looked through him and said "Yes," like Raleigh saying to the man who beheaded him, "Strike, man, strike!" Friends came to him under cover of night and told him he would be burned alive, as John Huss had been burned. Said Luther, "Though they kindle a fire whose flame should reach from Worms to Wittenberg, I would enter the jaws of the behemoth, break his teeth, and confess the Lord Jesus Christ." So they took their way on to Worms, down terror's highway; every bush and tree along the way might have been the screen of an assassin; every turn of the road ahead might be hiding a horseman with his hand upon his lance or sword. In the cool dawn of the sixteenth, a watchman on the roof of the Worms Cathedral blew his horn; Luther's wagon was coming through the gates, and all Worms was up to see it. There were thousands packing the narrow streets, and the wagon bounced slowly, at snail's pace, along the cobblestones to the house of the Knights of St. John. Here the traveler stepped down out of the straw, and looked over the sea of faces. He did not see Aleander, hidden there in the crush, who said afterward of the heretic, "Demons leaped from his eyes." Said Luther prayerfully to the people as he went into the house, "God will be with me."

As he sat down to breakfast in the morning, the Marshal of the Diet came to tell him that he was to face the Emperor at four that afternoon. He was ready at four. So crowded were the main streets, so full of hate and hope, that he cut across gardens and back yards to reach the Bishop's Palace. They kept him waiting for two long hours. He did not pace the floor. He did not tremble. This was the hour for which he had been born. At six he was led in; soldiers marched him in, closed the door behind him as they retired, like centurians leading in a martyr in the days of Nero. The room was filled with smoke, for it was growing dark and the lamps had just been lighted; through the haze, the one who stood alone could pick out white faces, gleaming eyes of friend and enemy, then human forms. There sat the Emperor, a boy of twenty-two, pale, half-interested, tired; Charles took his first long look at Martin Luther, judged him as kings do, all too rashly, decided, "He won't make a heretic of me." Arranged about the Emperor were six Electors, or rulers of his scattered German states, and six papal legates, among them Aleander. The Cardinal's lips were a tight white line; he said afterward that "The fool entered with a smile on his face." Luther looked at Charles, pitied him as a lamb among wolves; he met the glare of Aleander and thought to himself, "So the Jews must have looked at Christ." This was the moment of quiet before the clash, the moment in which the antagonists measured each other as gladiators had once measured the length of trident, the reach of arm, before they struck. At last it had come. The zero hour of Christianity!

A bench was piled high with Luther's books; pointing to them, an inquisitor, one Doctor Eck, asked Luther fiercely if they were his, and if he would here in the presence of the Emperor recant what he had said therein. The titles were read while Luther, taken aback by the sudden attack, gathered his wits. Yes, he admitted, they were his. But recant? He must have time to consider that. He could not peril God's word nor his own conscience by hasty answer. He begged for time to phrase it. Very well, said Eck; he could have time. He could have just twenty-four hours, and then he would either recant there before them all, or . . .

Luther needed no time to write that answer. This was fencing, the parrying of an unexpected blow. He knew what he would say, before his wagon entered Worms. That night he sat at his table in the inn and wrote in the light of a flickering candle to a friend: "This hour have I stood before the Emperor and the Diet, asked whether I would revoke my books. . . . Truly with Christ's aid I shall not revoke one jot or tittle." But the crowds in the streets of Worms did not know that. Outside, they watched the flickering light dance in Luther's window as men aboard a stricken ship watch a dim light on the shore.

At six on the second day he was again before the Diet. Aleander was not there this time; he sent word he would not listen to such a brazen heretic. Luther wore his black Augustinian gown; his head was shaved, after the fashion of the monks. He stood there firmly, waiting, one knee slightly bent in the direction of the Emperor. There was a quiet defiance in his eye, there was a rugged peasant's strength in his shoulders. He was young. Just thirty-eight. Young, for such business as this. Older men had been broken before such Councils, and . . . Eck shot a question at him: did he wish to defend *all* his books, or to retract *part* of them? Part, then? Rome would have been satisfied with that, with just an admission of *partial* heresy. It was a way out for Luther, a trap-door of a way out, and he saw it. Now he must answer, now settle it for himself, for Germany, for the world. Those crowds outside were waiting; the students and the professors back at Wittenberg were waiting; Germany, set afire by his bonfire, was watching him now; sickened Europe, restless to tear from her throat the garroting-cord of a Church gone bad . . . Europe waited. He was Europe's advocate before the bar of God. He knew it. He knew that if he weakened here, if he recanted, that there would be yet more years of weary struggle against this Church.

He knew that all the years gone were caught up in him. He was truth's Von Winkelried, gathering unto himself the spears of centuries of the enemies of God. The work of those dead and the hopes of those living hung on his reply; the tomorrow of the race lay in the hollow of his hand.

He spoke slowly, first in Latin and then in German. He said again the books were his; he told why he had written them, he classified them, he explained them. He once more assailed the Church and defended the Scriptures, but he said absolutely nothing of revoking anything he had ever said or written. As he finished, Eck leaped to his feet, his face livid: "Luther, you have not answered to the point. . . . *Will you recant or not?*" Plain as day, that question. Plain as death, the reasoning behind it. For Rome and Eck, there was but one issue here: this man must be silenced, must be forced to say that he had erred. He was not here to defend; he was not here to argue; he was not here to help lead anyone through the mists of bigotry to the mounts of truth. He was here only to admit that he was wrong, and that the Church was right. So, will you, or will you not . . . ?

Luther hesitated. The lamps pitched little daggers of light and shadow across the room; the silence of the place was an aching fire. The men of Rome leaned forward in their seats. Charles lifted his head from his hand and waited for the word that would wreck or weld his Empire. Luther looked slowly from Eck to the Emperor, and spoke deliberately the words that were the death-warrant of the old Rome and the birth-certificate of the Protestant Reformation:

"Since Your Majesty and your Lordships ask for a plain answer, I will give you one . . . Unless I am convinced by Scripture or by right reason, for I trust neither in popes nor in councils . . . unless I am thus convinced, I am bound by the text of the Bible, my conscience is captive to the word of God. I neither can nor will recant anything, since it is neither right nor safe to act against conscience. God help me. Amen."

Tumult split the smoke, like a screaming knife out of control; the council was a council no longer, but a bedlam. Eck stood rooted behind his desk, still shouting for recantation, recantation, though not a soul heard him. The Germans applauded, the Spaniards hissed, and the Italians pounded their desks and shook their fists in speechless Latin fury. The Emperor, disgusted and tired, rose abruptly and left the room. Luther saw quickly the futility of trying to say anything in this furor, turned and went out. The Spaniards followed him, crying, "Into the fire with him!" His loyal Germans formed a flying wedge about him, took him back to his quarters. There, he lifted his hands to heaven and sobbed out, "I am through. I am through!"

Of course, he was not through. He had won only his first major battle, and he was to fight and win many another before his work was done. Yet in this contest at Worms he had won the most important and decisive of them all. He had kept faith with those he had aroused against Rome, had stood fast when they could help him little, had convinced them that he was quite the leader they had thought him. Now they went at the work of reformation unafraid. Pope, Prince and Emperor no longer owned their souls; the pomp of that old dual power no longer sent these men to their knees; its threat of punishment and hell fell on deaf ears. Rome could bluster and threaten, but Rome might as well have saved her breath; Luther, heir to the courage and the faith of Huss, Savonarola and a thousand martyrs more, had thrown open a new, free Bible for men to feast their eyes upon, a new road to

Heaven for their feet to trod. He did not do it all; others started it, and threw the torch to him; still others finished, generations afterward, what he had begun. He was a Moses, leading his people out of bondage, setting their faces toward Canaan, giving them a new decalogue, then dying on the road. And every man alive today is a better man because Martin Luther lived, and rode that cart filled with straw, and stood at Worms.

Many a student has summed him up, by saying that he gave the world a new religion. That isn't enough to say of Martin Luther. He gave man a new soul.

VII

THE BATTLE OF BOSTON: ROGER WILLIAMS

MEN looked before they leaped in the Holy Commonwealth of Massachusetts Bay, and in fear of the Indians, the constables and God, they set a careful watch upon the words of their mouths, the meditations of their hearts and the habits of their neighbors. Perhaps the threat of the Indian was the worst; the musket over the fireplace was always primed and ready, and the houses of the colony were built within easy sprinting-distance of the thick-walled meeting-house, as much for safety's sake as for salvation's. Then there were the constables, the deputies, the strong arms of the law; they picked you up if you were on the streets after nine o'clock at night, fined you if they caught you drunk or kissing wife or sweetheart, gagged you at your own doorstep if you gossiped, led you to church if you dared absent yourself from service, could put you to death for blasphemy, adultery, idolatry or manstealing. (He who works on Sunday yet today breaks the law in Boston; also, he who swears!) Last but not least were the preachers, somber self-appointed representatives of God, who were the sentinels of the soul in the new land, who were ever alert for signs of heresy and falls from Puritan grace; they were the real, the absolute authority, the men-behind-the-law who used the civil officers to carry out their will; they regulated dress, speech, pleasure, manners, charity; they were the State; they dealt out more punishment than peace. They left not much chance for laughter. They made existence as stern and rockbound as their historic coast, and they never for an instant let anyone in Massachusetts forget that he was neatly trapped between the Indians, the preachers, the devil and the deep blue sea.

It wasn't that they wanted it that way; self-preservation commanded it. Let the vigil against the red man lag, and some dawn might find their cabins a line of smoking ruins on the shore. Let the preacher grow lax and doubt and disbelief and discord would creep into the Church, the strong rock on which the house of State was built. They could tolerate no innovator, no man who would trifle with their government or faith; this was no place for radicals, dissenters, cranks or men with independent minds. Puritanism was a closed shop; you either did as the Puritans did, or you got out. You got out to Plymouth, that Pilgrim colony of rascals who had turned their backs forever on the Church of England to which Boston clung. Or you might go to Salem, which had not turned its back so completely, and which religiously stood somewhere between Plymouth and the Bay. Or you could go out in the woods and live with the Indians. There were plenty of woods.

Such a place was Massachusetts Bay on that cold morning in 1631 when the good ship *Lyon* dropped anchor off Nantasket, a barren, frozen, perilous land ruled by men of blood-and-iron. A hardy bark, this *Lyon;* she had fought her way for two bitter winter months through icy seas, through storm and death-laden gale. She came to rest in a bay of drifting ice, and her rigging hung heavy with frozen spray. In her hold lay two hundred tons of supplies: seeds, bullets, shovels, Bibles, drugs, denim and dishes. On her decks shivered twenty passengers, chilled to the bone and thanking God for sight o' land. Down in his cabin a young minister awaited the reception committee; he was the most notable man aboard, a gallant rebel on the run before the wrath of His Majesty King James and therefore loved in advance by all in the Bay. He came recommended by friend and enemy alike as "a good friend, a good man and a godly young minister, passionate and precipitate and divinely mad." With him came Mary, his young bride, who thought him divine but hardly mad.

The folk of the Bay cheered him ashore, and they made much of him at the great public feast of thanksgiving on February twenty-second. All eyes were on him, as all eyes in that day and place were always on the minister; Napoleonesque, wherever he sat at that table was the head of the table. Goodly. Godly. Young. Courageous. Eloquent. Inspired. A rebel fit to live with rebels, and lead them: this they saw in him, and this they loved. But . . . Passionate. Precipitate. Independent, and ready to fight for his independence. A fighter. Fiery. Explosive! A man with a troubled spirit who never once had said, "Be still, my soul." A man, as Cotton Mather came later to describe him, "with a windmill in his mind." A man as far ahead of these colonists in his quest for peace and the truth of God as the Wright brothers were ahead of the rider of the horse-and-buggy, as Edison was ahead of the kerosene lamp. Boston did not see this man in Roger Williams, did not see this stranger at their feast. They were shocked when they discovered how shortsighted they had been.

It did not take them long to discover it. It was a matter of days when a delegation from the Church in Boston came knocking on Mr. Williams' door. They came bearing a great gift. Their teacher in religion, the Reverend John Wilson, was about to return to England, and, in council assembled, they had settled upon the good and godly Roger as his successor. They extended their invitation, and sat back, knowing of course that the young man would stagger and stammer as the import of it dawned upon him. Of course, he'd jump at it; this was the ecclesiastical prize of the new world, offered to a raw youth hardly out of the frigid cabin of the *Lyon*. They blinked as the amazing young man told them quietly that he was not interested, that he could not accept such a position until they changed their ways in Boston, until they became clearly "a separated people" from the despised Church of England, and until they separated Church from State in their colony. If they'd do that, he might think about it. If he'd slapped them in the face, they couldn't have been more surprised. Mary, listening, held a hand over her heart.

But ... Mr. Williams ... this is Boston! Don't you understand? This is the First Church of America, with all the First Families and all the best people in her pews. This is the opportunity of a lifetime. Think of the prestige ... Yes, yes, Mr. Williams had thought of all that. But he thought more of peace than of prestige, more of first principles than of First Families. He'd crossed three thousand miles of icy brine for these principles of his, searching for a land and a state where men were honestly free and able to worship the Almighty as they saw fit. He'd broken forever with State Churches; he'd come this far to find "soul liberty," or room for his soul to grow, and he didn't intend to compromise. That was first, to him. That was insanity, to the delegation; they left his house, and they never entered it again. The young upstart! Did he expect them to turn the colony inside out, just to suit him? Him, and his soul liberty! If this was the way he felt about things, he'd better move on.

He moved. He left Boston and the Bay. There was an

opening for a minister in Salem, and to Salem Roger Williams took his stormy way, throwing over his shoulder a few parting vitriolic remarks about the manner in which the civil authorities in the Bay were allowed to punish spiritual offenses, and about how wrong it was that a man was forced to be a church-member before he could be a citizen. Salem had her tongue in her cheek when she called him; this was a chance to show her disdain of Boston, on whom she lavished no love. The General Court of Boston sent a letter warning Salem against the windmill-man, but Salem laughed, put Roger Williams in charge at once and rejoiced that now they had a leader who would lead them against the overbearing General Court and in the general direction of the mercy-seat, however noisily.

That was in the spring of 1631; by the end of the summer, Roger Williams was in trouble in Salem. He had gone the limit in his preaching; he was a bit *too* outspoken about Boston; he stood for such a radical separation of Church and State, and he threw out such bolshevistic homiletic bombs that even Salem became alarmed. They weren't ready for this, yet; it was better to go slowly with such ideas, counseled their elders. Better move on, Roger Williams. He moved on. He moved to the only place left to move to. To Plymouth.

Now Plymouth, suspect as it was of being "Separatist," was not that at all. As a matter of fact, there was no Separatist Church, in the rigid sense, anywhere in New England. And there was as much persecution for non-conformity in Plymouth as elsewhere, and as little real religious liberty, and as solid a union of civil and ecclesiastical powers. But there was also a more pronounced dislike for the Church of England and all her episcopal works; there were many in

Plymouth who hated even the name of that Church, and who would no more think of going back to her than they would have thought of going back to England. They were *more* separated here than anywhere else in New England, and Roger Williams went to them gladly. Surely, here he could preach what he wanted to preach, without hindrance. Mary wondered about that . . .

He divided his time between the Indians and the whites. He went to take the gospel to the red man a full fourteen years before John Eliot appeared upon the scene; God, he said, "pleased to give me a painful patient spirit to lodge with them in their filthy smoke holes . . ." and he came to thank God for it, soon afterward. For things did not go so well in Plymouth as he expected. The Pilgrims gasped at some of the things he said to them. Such outlandish things, such unusual things. He went so far, one Sabbath, as to say that the whole of New England was founded on a lie . . . the lie that the Colonists really had a right to the land they were living on. The Indians owned the land, said Roger Williams; the colonies had stolen it. But didn't they have a patent, a charter from the King? Not worth the parchment it was written on, said the preacher: had the King paid the Indians for the land? He had not! Therefore the King had never owned it, either. Shame on you, Plymouth, for your dishonesty. And shame on you for this miserable union of Church and State. Shame on you for . . . Ere long the good Governor Bradford was writing in his diary that Mr. Williams was "a man godly and zealous, having many precious ‚parts, but very unsettled in judgments . . . I hope he belongs to the Lord!" The difficulty was, of course, that Bradford and Williams represented two vastly different schools of thought; the Governor was a conservative, clinging to the old; the preacher was a radical, thinking of the new. One wanted to hold fast to what he had, in government and policy of Church; the other wanted to seize on something new. Bradford was a child of his hour; the chief sin of Roger Williams was that he was too far ahead of his hour. It was a dilemma, solved only when Salem, mercifully and unaccountably, asked him to come back and preach there a second time.

He went joyfully. Salem knew him, and Salem wanted him! General Court, in Boston, advised Salem that no good would come of this, but only "ill consequence"; General Court may have sensed the fact that this second call to Salem was the beginning of the end, the prelude of the most violent controversy ever to shake the colony. Williams was more violent than ever now; he preached furiously against the theft of land from the Indians; he went the limit in demanding the separation of civil and religious powers, the end of civil interference in ecclesiastical and Church affairs; he refused to take the oath of submission to the authority of the General Court and he demanded that Salem, Plymouth and Boston alike become immediately a clearly "separated people." He was an agitator, a disturber without a peer; wherever he went, there were trouble and turmoil. No need for a beadle to keep folks awake when he preached; those who sat in his pews sat up straight, wondering what was coming next. He raged against the "idolatry" of the presence of a cross in the English flag, which flew from the blockhouses; shortly after the sermon, John Endicott drew his sword in the street and hacked out the cross. And shortly after that, General Court went into action. This was the last straw; the colony needed the aid of England, depended on the help in Parliament of such men as Warwick, Pym and Hampden, and this was flagrant insult to the English. The Court stepped in, put Roger Williams "on probation" for a year. It was a suspended sentence, a warning; Williams was under a cloud. He never saw the cloud. He never paid the slightest heed to his "probation." Do what they would, he would not be still; he had started this, and he would finish it. He resigned from his pulpit, rather than embarrass the Church; he was a preacher without a pulpit, a clergyman without a congregation. He was the first rebel against the New England Church; he was the symbol of dissent. No one, not even Mary, dared guess what the end might be. Mary went each Sunday to sit in her pew at the church, where she maintained her membership. Roger Williams never interfered with her in that; he believed in religious liberty, and that liberty began at home. She went to church; he stayed at home, preaching and teaching impromptu to whoever came to hear him. A good many came. So many came that General Court, its patience at last exhausted, summoned him to appear in Newtown, for "trial." This was 1634. Roger Williams had been in the colony just four years; in that time he had fomented a revolution, had forced into the open a consideration of the most important problem in the history of the American people.

For truth's and history's sake, let's get this straight: what was on trial that day in Newtown was not a man but a principle. The real question before the Court was not "What shall we do with Roger Williams?", but rather what they should do with what Roger Williams stood for. Not what was going to happen to the rebel, but what was going to happen to religion in America, was the issue. This day was the cause of liberty haled to the bar; this day it was to be decided whether conformity or free conscience were to rule the land; this day was it to be determined whether you and I were to worship, pray, and believe as we chose, or as the magistrates and governors and mayors dictated. Roger Williams, in rebellion against dictation, was only the hapless individual in whom the issue came to a head; he was but an instrument, a human instrument, in the hand of God. If he could stand and deliver now for God, then posterity would be free; if he failed, if he broke down, if he became in the heat of the battle a Benedict Arnold, then . . . well, what then?

Court met in Thomas Hooker's Church in Newtown (we call it Cambridge today), a bare, bleak, Puritan church, coldly Calvinistic. There was a dirt floor and there were wooden benches for pews, stiff and hard. There was no heat in Thomas Hooker's Church, and this was October. On the benches sat fifty fathers of the Commonwealth, fifty hardened, seasoned, storm-tried men who had torn their living from the rocky soil and staked their lives and destinies in a cold and hostile land. At their head sat Governor Haynes, patrician, pompous, petty, petulant, responsible to the King for peace and progress overseas. Nearest him sat the magistrates, Thomas Dudley, William Coddington, John Winthrop and his son John, and five others not so well-known to later fame. There were twenty-five deputies. There were all the other ministers of the colony, come to see justice done and the plague ended. Watching the ministers, among the spectators, was a bearded little man in a skullcap: this was John Endicott, demoted and in disgrace for hacking at the flag, close friend of the man on trial and utterly unable to speak a word in his defense. Among the preachers sat John Cotton, who had known Williams in England; Thomas Hooker, shortly to leave for the Connecticut Valley in protest against the very men now about to punish Roger Williams. Hooker and Cotton were also friends of the rebel. Cotton was the only man to disapprove of what the Court did that day; Hooker tried his best to make his friend recant, and "see the error of his ways!"

There was no trial; Roger Williams was no more on trial here than Jesus had been before Pilate, or Luther before Charles V. Every man in the church had long since made up his mind about the culprit. There were no jury, no formal charges, no indictments, no judge, except as all present, from the Governor down to the meanest magistrate, were at once judge, jury and prosecuting attorney combined. All they did was to read out the list of errors Williams had committed, and pass sentence. Confronted with the list, Roger Williams said yes, he had been guilty of all of it; asked if he would recant and bow to the authority of the Court (is this Newtown, or Worms?) he said plainly, "No!" Hooker reasoned with him, argued with him; he might as well have tried to reason with the North Star or the north wind. There was no recanting in him, no regret, no turning back. Hooker threw up his hands. A hush fell. This was the climax. The Governor rose, looked long at Roger Williams, began reading from a legal document. Williams looked away from him, out of the window, at scarlet leaves falling from the trees outside, through the crisp October air. Luther had his cheering Europe at his back; even Jesus had his James and John and his Simon of Cyrene. But of all the rebel-pioneers of history, Roger Williams is the most deserted and alone. He had no one, save Mary. And Mary could not come. . . .

The Governor droned on, recounting again the sins of the accused, coming at last to this: ". . . Mr. Williams shall depart out of this jurisdiction within six weeks next ensuing . . . not to return any more without license from the Court."

Banished! Mr. Williams rose without a word and walked out of the church. No man looked at him.

He went home. He was a sick man, worn of body and weary of mind. He told Mary. That was difficult, harder than facing the ordeal at Newtown, for Mary was soon to become a mother. Mary took it calmly, but her eyes asked, "Where now?" Salem took it not so calmly as Mary; Salem, now that the harm had been done, was mad. Salem was so mad that the Court grew suddenly merciful: Mr. Williams need not go until the baby had arrived, until the snows of winter had melted, until he had recovered from his illness. But Mr. Williams, through the winter, would behave himself. He was not to preach, not to hold any meetings in his house, not to teach his heresy to anyone nor "go about to draw others to his opinion." (So he had been banished not for any crime, but for an opinion!) He'd behave himself, keep the peace, and with the warm winds of spring, get out.

The baby came; they named her Freeborn, as in further defiance of the Court. Mary kept one foot on the cradle, one eye on her husband. Visitors were coming, regularly, to her house; at first they came singly, then by twos and threes. They came, they lingered, they talked far into the night. The town knew all about it, immediately; Boston heard of it. This was treason: Roger Williams was drawing members away from the Church, and the Church was the State. He had broken his parole, and now the Court struck swiftly. It was dramatic. Up the street marched Captain Underhill, from Boston, with fourteen good men and strong at his back; they knocked on Roger Williams' door. Mary opened the door, and stood there with Freeborn in her arms. Mr. Williams . . . they had a warrant for the arrest of Mr. Williams. Mary smiled and shook her head. Mr. Williams was not at home. Where was he? Really, she did not know. Well, then, how long had he been gone? Three days, said Mrs. Williams. She closed the door. Valiant Captain Underhill and his fourteen men marched down the street again. The rascal had slipped through their fingers. He was gone. Gone, they knew not where.

He was gone beyond their reach, gone floundering through the forest snow to the wigwam of Massasoit, to the only haven he had left this side of Heaven, to the "filthy smoke holes" of the Indians. Gone to found Providence, a city of refuge for all dissenters, a city with gates wide open to all who searched for God and truth and who found Puritanism too small a house for their souls to live in. It was the first city of its kind in the New World. It was a city set on a hill, where no ears were cropped in the interests of conformity nor Quakers whipped at cart-tails in their quest of Inner Light. (Williams never liked the Quaker, but he never persecuted him.) A city on a hill whose light could not be hid, in whose bright light was born the epochal and revolutionary provisions which flowered at last in these words, in the Constitution of the United States:

"... no religious test shall ever be required as a qualification to any office or public trust under the United States."

"Congress shall make no law respecting an establishment of religion, or prohibiting the free exercise thereof; ..."

We got that from Roger Williams. It was blown down to us from the "man with a windmill in his mind." Rebel and outcast to his Puritian contemporaries, he has become to us a

Galahad of God who fought singlehanded and alone, that day in Thomas Hooker's Church in Newtown.

Martin Luther gave us the right to be Protestant; Roger Williams gave us the right to be any kind of Protestant. The German freed us from an intolerable Catholicism; the firebrand of Salem freed us from a Puritan theocracy almost as bad. When he won this battle of Boston by allowing himself to be banished, he established himself as the true father of the American dream: the dream of a really free commonwealth in which all of us are on equal footing before God and the law, all entitled to life, liberty and the pursuit of happiness, all free to search for the truth as we see fit to search, and in finding it to find emancipation, political and social and religious, for our hearts and minds and souls.

VIII

STREET BATTLE: GEORGE WHITEFIELD

THERE was an old woman, worn and wrinkled with poverty and years, who sold apples to the boys at Oxford. She was as much a campus fixture as the Dean, and the boys enjoyed her; they prodded her into cackling, cronish laughter, and they liked the way she rubbed the apples bright on her old apron, and they smiled at her tearful tales of how hard life was in the slums. They had enough to worry about, with their lectures and examinations and vacations, without the slums. So they munched her apples and forgot her poverty. All England did that.

One fateful evening in the year of our Lord 1732, this "Apple Annie" climbed a flight of ancient stairs at Pembroke College and rapped humbly on the door of one Charles Wesley, student. Abject and apologetic for disturbing such a fine young man, she wiped a tear from her eye with a dirty ragged sleeve and begged a favor of him. A friend of hers, a poor woman in prison, had tried to kill herself and . . . failed. Would Mr. Wesley, or some other of the boys in that Holy Club, go to the workhouse and pray with her? Why, yes, Mr. Wesley would go, himself. But why had she come to him? Who had sent her? Apple Annie did not want to say; she'd promised. . . . Well, if Mr. Wesley insisted, it was that Mr. Whitefield had sent her. She shuffled down the stairs and out into the night and anonymity, and probably to the potter's field, never dreaming that she had brought together two men who were to make the world tremble and rejoice.

So George Whitefield had sent her, mused Charles Wesley as he closed his door. Wesley knew him, vaguely: Whitefield was a campus eccentric, a highly emotional religious extremist, a youth with a tortured soul and mind who was going through hell in search of God. He walked the campus moodily, with his eyes on the ground and his hands clasped behind his back. He took Communion weekly, at St. Mary's Church, sitting apart, a good-looking young giant with a splendid body and a courteous, reserved demeanor. He had a reputation for piety. Charles Wesley sent him an invitation to breakfast, next morning. Charles introduced him to his brother, John. Within the week, Whitefield was a member of the Holy Club.

The men in the Holy Club liked him, but . . . his buoyancy, his fierce energy were disturbing. George Whitefield was to the Holy Club what a chirping cricket is to a quiet chapel. The Wesleys were quiet-chapel spirits; John was a mystic; Charles, a composer of hymns. Whitefield was explosive, impetuous, now hot and now cold, now pacing the floor and shouting, now in a trance with his eyes closed. He was a creature of ecstasy, revelations, whispers and thunderings; his voice held the sonorous rumble of a Salvation Army drum. And he was wholly lovable. He would walk alone for long hours in the fields, or lie alone long hours under the trees or on his study floor, with his arms stretched out to form a cross, sobbing: yet no man rebuked him, or scolded him. He would expose himself to winter cold until the flesh of his back and arms turned blue and then black; he ate the coarsest food when he might have eaten the best—hard bread, strong tea without sugar; he wore a shabby coat, refused to powder his hair, fasted until he staggered with weakness, found himself in a sparkling heaven of faith at sunrise and in a misery of fear and faithlessness at sunset, yet they honored him in the Holy Club, and longed to help him. As they came to know him and his background, their admiration of him knew no bounds.

For this struggling, tortured Whitefield had lived a life of struggle and torture. He had been kicked and cuffed and cursed at and abused for the faith that was in him; fit for Heaven, he had fought for his life and his soul in a pig-sty. To be exact, in a barroom. George Whitefield, before he came to make Oxford famous, had been a pot-boy in a Glouchester tavern. Tapster and the son of a tapster at Bell Inn, he served beer and ale and bitters to his roaring betters, repulsed by their blasphemy and ribaldry, slipping off to his garret room at night to read his Bible. He dreamed of better days. He envied the local parish minister, and he vowed that one day he would leave the dirty, stinking Bell and walk in the clean air with God. He hated his job; he despised those he served; he knew what it meant to be poor, "lower class"; he lived with the lowest, and felt on his back their stripes of pain and in his heart the aching fire of their smoldering rebellion and their sweet dreams of release. Some day, this multitude of the maltreated would be set free, would rise up and claim their share of life and liberty.

The mark of that multitude was on him, plain as the mark of Cain. He knew men, women and children who had been crowded into prisons that had no sewers or water supply; he saw them carried dead out of those dungeons, dead of jail fever. He knew of men who had been kidnaped by the press-gang; he knew of women who had fought off starvation by stealing or counterfeiting, and been hanged for it, at Tyburn.

He saw playmates tied to the whipping-post, taking cruel beatings for some rich young man who paid the whipping-boy to suffer for his sins; he saw the thirsty poor drink muddy water from the gutters. He knew that the funerals of the poor were often drunken orgies, with no religious burial service worthy of the name. His half lived that way; no, his three-quarters lived that way. And the other, upper quarter . . . he knew them too. He saw rich men in lace shirts and ruffles kiss each other in the street; he saw rich and haughty ladies splash mud all over everybody as they rode by in coaches drawn by six horses with postillions; he knew that foppish beaux along the Strand would pay forty guineas for a wig; he knew that the over-lords of England subscribed to cricket-clubs and the Thirty-Nine Articles of Religion and sat in carved oak pews at the cathedral, while the under-dogs, like himself, had hardly a cheap wooden cross in a wooden shack to kneel to. He knew that bands of "Mohocks" and "Hawkubites" robbed and murdered in bright daylight in Grosvenor Square and Piccadilly; he knew that England had been robbed of something during this reign of His Majesty George II, something more valuable than silver and gold and precious stones. Of high faith, and of that moral strength that had made her strong and great. Of brotherhood, and charity, and faith in God and man. He knew that those over-lords of the upper quarter, in charge of Church and counting-house and court of law, meant to keep things just that way. He knew that the man who spoke out for the masses against the classes did so at his peril.

Marked as he was, concerned as he was for the pauper and the poor, even this Whitefield did not speak for them at first; as a matter of record, before he was out of Oxford he had become the pet of the aristocracy; in the early days he was more the prodigy of wealth than the people's prophet. He visited the poor and he prayed with the prisoner, from honest motives purely; but this was accepted by his contemporaries more as expected gestures than as a life-work. It was his preaching that attracted attention from the high and the lowly alike. "He preached like a lion!" cried one of his hearers after his first sermon. Downy-cheeked, still an under-graduate, he became a pulpit sensation overnight. He was the boy-wonder of the clergy. Society lionized him; he was their current, passing rage. At sixteen he had been a tapster, and at twenty-five he was the most famous preacher in England. Lady Huntington went to hear him, and reported to her courtly circle: "His lips drooped like the honey-comb and were a well of life." The cynical Horace Walpole was charmed, in spite of himself; the foppish and fashionable Lord Chesterfield complimented him; David Garrick, the greatest actor of the century, envied him his voice and his sense of the dramatic. He drew audiences of hundreds, then thousands; he made them laugh, he made them moan, he swayed them like reeds in the wind. A surly old general who despised preachers followed the crowd, listened as the boy-wonder described a blind man stumbling nearer and nearer to the edge of a precipice, forgot himself and his preacher-hate and shouted right out in meeting: "Good God, he's over."

The youthful phenomenon preached no scholarly sermons, for he was no scholar. He preached something above scholar-ship: regeneration. Regeneration, and conversion. Sudden, instantaneous, transforming, Damascus-road conversion. He talked much of being born again. (He taught this and he experienced this three long years before the Wesleys taught or felt it.) His texts were ". . . He hath perfected them that are sanctified," and "If any man be in Christ he is a new creature," and "God hath chosen the weak things of the world to confound the things which are mighty." He preached that to the mighty classes who ignored Christ, to the weak masses who were denied Christ. He was spectacular, emotional, inspirational, somehow supernatural. High church parsons looked and listened and became suspicious of his quick success; one called him "a pragmatical rascal," and when he published a little pamphlet entitled *A Short Account of God's Dealings with the Reverend George Whitefield, B.A.*, the shocked Bishop of Exeter called it "such a boyish, ludicrous, filthy, nasty and shameless relation of himself, as quite defiles paper, and is shocking to decency and modesty." But nobody paid much attention to that; thousands crowded in to hear him, packing the churches to suffocation, fighting for a place at open door or window. Perhaps they all had nasty and shameless and indecent and immodest "relations" in their own lives which the well-meaning Bishop of Exeter had not much helped them to cast off.

In 1736, a call came to Whitefield from John Wesley: "Come to Georgia, and help us." Poor John Wesley! Ardent, disciplining, stiff-necked churchman, he had gone to Georgia to save the Indians and convert the whites; he was the last man in England to try that. Oxford-reared, scholarly, cultured, he found himself miscast in the wilderness, where scholarship and culture were for the time wasted; he left uncouth Georgia cold, and sent for the fiery Whitefield to come and do what he couldn't do. To the dismay of those who were loving and lionizing George Whitefield in England, he went. Here's irony: Whitefield sailed out of harbor in England the same day that Wesley sailed in! He seemed as glad to go as Wesley was to come home; all the way over, on shipboard, he was preaching to the officers on deck, or going below to pray with the men in the steerage. Arrived in Georgia, he sought out those most in need of his preaching, and preached as though the thought of failure had never entered his head. That may be one reason why he won in Georgia, where Wesley had so miserably failed. Strong as the strongest man in the colony, gifted with a voice that could outshout a forest storm and with a personal knowledge (gained in the school of experience) of what the unlettered man of the masses was thinking and feeling and wanting in his life, Whitefield succeeded. He was one of them; he spoke their language; he shook them. He realized now that he could preach anywhere, that he must preach everywhere; God, he felt, had never intended him to be a parish priest, moving in a tiny circle; God had not made him to found any little sect, but to range as a free-lance Prometheus bearing fire from Heaven to all nations. The earth was his parish.

He founded schools in Georgia, for the poor; he founded an orphanage, and within six months' time was scurrying back to England to raise money to take care of his orphans. It was a fearful passage. He sat in his dark cabin, wrapped in a buffalo-hide, listening to the wind rip the sails to shreds overhead, hearing the tackle break; the roar of the storm was sweet music to his tumult-riven soul; there was no fear in him. He sat there planning his next move against the sin of England and telling himself that he must raise money, somehow, for the Georgia orphanage. And that he must somehow reach the colliers, workers, paupers, while he raised it.

Had he known what waited for him at home, he might have stayed in Georgia. England should have welcomed him with open arms, if his success in Georgia and his earlier success in England meant anything at all. But . . . England did not take him to her heart. This was not the England he had left six short months ago. There was a chill in the air. Something was wrong, awry. That little Holy Club had broken up and scattered, its members preaching the thoughts and experiences they had thought and experienced at college; they were growing in England's mind from a shadow no larger than the hand of a man to a national nuisance; let out of their cloistered halls, let loose upon the populace, they had stirred a pretty mess. They "stirred madness in the people"; they stirred the ecclesiastical drones in quiet parishes, and the drones began to buzz in angry protest. For the drones had been having an easy time of it, preaching ivy-covered sermons in ivy-covered churches, preaching lovely little essays that dealt vaguely with a vague morality and a blind allegiance to His Majesty the King. Into their midst now came the Holy Clubbers, striking fire in the quiet places with wild talk of conversion, regeneration, being born again, being made furiously alive again with a burning passion for souls and the soul of England. They swung their evangelical clubs at the smug complacency of the pulpit and the pew; they spoke out against the laxity in morality and religion which was responsible for the lowest moral and religious state that England had ever known. They made this smug and sleeping religion look like what it was: a farce. They were calling people back to Church on the Sabbath, from the bear-pit and the tavern. They objected to the Sabbath being kept a saturnalia, to sin remaining a sovereign more powerful than the King. They called on England to awake, to save herself, to turn from social sin to personal salvation, to put on again the whole armor of Christ before the battle was forever lost to the hosts of hell. They were agitators. And who likes an agitator, especially when one is asleep? The sleepers stirred, grumbled, objected. The quiet parsons and those who paid pew-rents to keep them quiet, set themselves against the Oxford disturbers, and resolved either to quiet them or be rid of them. Said Bishop Butler to John Wesley, "You have no business here; you are not commissioned to preach in this parish; Therefore I advise you to go hence."

Such men as Wesley, said the Bishop and his friends, were dangerous; they were "enthusiasts," and to be enthusiastic was to be undignified, and perhaps morally "unsound," or at least "indifferent to the conventional standards of society." They were defying the traditions of the Church; they shouted when they preached; they actually made extemporaneous prayers, without the aid of the Book of Common Prayer! They played on the emotions. They were rabble-rousers, like the Quakers and the Muggletonians and the Fifth Monarchy men and the Anabaptists. The Church just would not stand for it. The Church closed its doors to such preaching and such men, blissfully unaware that a revolution was being born in the cellar of the Church, and that they were on the eve of one of the world's great decisive battles. But those loyal to the status-quo seldom try to see things through the eyes of the rebel, before the rebel gets the upper hand. They simply say, "Be still, or get out!" They said that to the Wesleys and their friends. They barred them from their pulpits and made them outlaws, men with much to say to England and no place to say it. Charles Wesley tried to say it in the open air, and found himself called on the carpet by his Bishop, and threatened with excommunication. Brother John Wesley, loving the Church and hesitating to desert it, hesitated. Where now? They stood at a crossroads and waited, and while they waited, Whitefield came.

George Whitefield found himself forced to join the Wesleys at this crossroads; he found himself identified, the day he stepped ashore, with these enthusiasts. He was one of them, perhaps the worst of them, for he had the loudest voice. His old friend, Bishop Benson, said of him, "Though mistaken on some points, I think Mr. Whitefield a pious, well-meaning young man. . . ." That was damning with faint praise; others went further and damned openly. Others slammed doors in his face, and refused him a place from which to unleash his clarion voice. Multitudes waited to hear him; there were still crowds wherever he went. But there were fewer and fewer places where he might go. And day by day, he was reminded in no uncertain terms that he was no longer a lion but a leper. He stared at those closed doors, and he raged. Disgusted, he turned his back on London and went down to Bristol.

Things would be better in Bristol; he had preached to thousands there, eighteen months ago, and people hadn't forgotten that. But . . . some people, some important people, had forgotten that, or else remembered it too well. There was the sound of closing doors in Bristol; there was the icy shoulder of the Church, as in London. Whitefield tried to comfort himself with preaching a sermon in prison, on "The Penitent Thief." (He took a collection in that prison for the Orphanage, and he got fifteen shillings!) The last straw fell on his sturdy back when the State-Church authorities informed the jailer that this Whitefield was to preach no more to the prisoners. Why? Well, he talked too much about their "being born again."

Now Whitefield stopped, looked, listened, and decided. Here he was with his Gospel of regeneration as a fire shut up in his bones. Here were the thousands and tens of thousands of multitudes, waiting; they as well as he had been locked out of the churches. There was only one question for him to face, for him to settle. Were they to stay locked out? Were they to accept this as they had accepted the gibbet and the whipping-post and the press-gang? It was not "Who is right, Mr. Whitefield or the parsons?" It was, "Are these hungry to be fed, or are they to be ignored?" Shall it be saturnalia or salvation? Should Whitefield stand before them as a lion of the Lord, or should he bow his neck to the episcopal yoke, and go like a lamb to be slaughtered into ineffectiveness? Should these poor whom he had learned to love in his days at Bell Inn be starved in soul as well as in body? Should England slide on down, deeper, deeper, deeper, or should England awake and stretch every nerve and in the warm sun of his burning gospel take on new strength and hope and power? Which, George Whitefield? Which, England and the Church?

Can anyone imagine that there was ever a doubt in George Whitefield's mind as to what he should do? What does a fighter do when battle looms? He fights! So Whitefield, in one of the greatest crises that ever faced him and his Englishmen, resolved to fight, though he fought alone and against everybody. Throwing caution to the winds, striking out in solitary fury at those who sought to silence him by turning rusty keys in old church doors, he picked out the most hostile spot in England to begin his fight, and began there. He walked four miles out of Bristol, to Kingswood; to a deserted race-track, to a wild, brutal, no-man's land where timid preachers never dared to show their faces; to a ribald, drunken crowd of colliers who lived in filth and faithlessness and fighting ferment; to the most ignorant and savage and forgotten of all Englishmen . . . he went there, and he preached to them, *in the open air!*

[115]

England was thunderstruck at the news. Preaching to colliers, and to colliers' wives! Why, no one paid any attention to that crowd; not, that is, until money and food ran short in Kingswood, and the colliers marched into town to take what they wanted by brute force. And here was George Whitefield, the boy-wonder who had fascinated Chesterfield and who had been envied by Garrick, *preaching* to them, putting in their savage hands the dynamite of a liberating, regenerating gospel. Preaching in the fields, in the open air, in defiance of the Church! He was exciting these forgotten ones, making them weep and making them moan; they fell to the ground under his inspired oratory, screaming for mercy and shouting for joy. The worst of it was, there was no way of stopping it; it may have been irregular, and untraditional, but it was not illegal. The Prayer Book had nothing against it, even if the preachers did.

The audiences grew, in Kingswood and round about. There were twoscore listeners to that first sermon; there were ten thousand two days later; within three weeks, the audience covered three acres. New creatures walked the streets of Kingswood and Bristol; "saved" creatures they called themselves. As they multiplied, and as Whitefield found himself faced by more and yet more thousands, he sent for help. He sent for John Wesley. Wesley demurred. He was still a loyal priest in the Church of England, even though the Church would not listen to him, nor have him in her pulpits. Should he follow Whitefield out of the Church, or not? He closed his eyes, opened his Bible, placed his finger at random on a text that he thought might help him decide; he read, "Get thee up into the mountain . . ." That was plain enough. He tried once more; this time it was, "And the children of Israel wept for Moses in the plains of Moab thirty days . . ."

That was plain, too. Still hesitant, he decided to draw lots to see whether he or some other "Methodist" should go; he drew the fatal slip. He packed his saddlebags and rode for Bristol. His heart was in revolt against all this, even yet. Preach in the fields, in the *streets!* It was . . . vulgar. But he went. On Saturday night he listened to Whitefield preach in the open air, and he shuddered; his sensitive soul still "thought the saving of souls almost a sin if it had not been done in a church." On Sunday he consented to talk to them in a house on Nicholas Street. On Monday he capitulated: "I submitted to be more vile, and proclaimed in the highways . . . to about three thousand people." His text: "The Spirit of the Lord is upon me, because He hath anointed me to preach the gospel to the poor." John Wesley had been won, and the great Wesleyan Revival, to last more than forty years, had begun.

The "battle of the streets" was on in earnest as Wesley followed Whitefield out into the open air. To the ranks of the wealthier pew-renters and worried parsons was added a new enemy: the poor themselves. (That's always the hardest part of revival and reform: often those who need it most fight it hardest.) Urged by the classes, the masses fought Wesley and Whitefield in the streets; there were hecklers, drunks, even assassins. "Knock his brains out," "Kill him," vied with "Amen" and "Praise the Lord!" There were sticks and stones and wild words thrown; blood was drawn on the head of many a preacher, but the preachers preached on. At Poole, you may still read on the church records an entry of the "score" or debt at the local inn for drinks furnished to the mob "for driving out the Methodists." Chapels where they preached were razed, burned, wrecked; inns where they slept were set afire. They were denounced as papists, traitors, lunatics; they were stoned, clubbed, stabbed. They were never once dismayed. From Kingswood and Bristol they spread their nets all over England; they gathered scores, hundreds, thousands into their nets and held them there for God. And their nets, so heavy with the miraculous draught, seemed like to break beneath the strain. Happily, they held; the break came elsewhere, in the Church. Emptier and emptier became the pews, in spite of every effort to stem the tide; out into the streets, out into the fields went England, out into churchyards to hear the enthusiasts. When the Church at last realized that this thing could not be stopped, the Church surrendered. When the poor realized what was happening to them, the poor surrendered too and surged up to the mourner's bench. And more often than not, at the bench, they found at their sides men and women in silks and ruffles. There, social distinctions and the divisions of class and mass were providentially overcome: while the proletarians of France, across the Channel, tried to solve their problem by hustling the aristocrats to the guillotine, the poor of England knelt with *their* aristocrats at the mourner's bench. There, bloodlessly, in quickened faith and not in terror, was their battle won and the new liberty, equality and fraternity announced.

This was the Wesleyan Revival; it bears the name of the little Oxford don whom Methodists by the million, all over the world, are proud to call father. That is meet and right and as it should be, for had there been no John Wesley, with his brother Charles, there might have been no organized Methodism. He it was who bound the thing together, as sticks in a bundle; he gave it form and unity. Whitefield admitted that, himself: "This [organizing] I neglected, and my people were a rope of sand." George Whitefield was no organizer; aside from joining his first few Welsh converts into a General Association of Methodists, and setting up a local-preacher movement, he did little or no organizing. That was not his forte. He was a thunderbolt; it was not for him to sit in stuffy council-rooms planning, reasoning why or why not, electing officers or reading the minutes of the last meeting. He was born not to plan the battle but to lead the charge. He had to be preaching, spreading the fire, gathering crowds and swaying them. He did that well, in England and America. He left it to those who followed him to keep the thrill alive by incorporating it into a Society, or Church.

Yet we abuse his memory when we forget that he brought about this revival by literally shoving John Wesley into the streets. In that crucial moment when the whole Methodist movement wavered in uncertainty, it was the ex-pot-boy from Bell Inn who led the leaders out to the mining-pits and the race-tracks and the curbstones. It was Whitefield who saved Wesley from the fate of unknown parish priest, who galvanized him into action as a world-awakener who could cry "The world is my parish!" And when Whitefield did that, he brought not only Wesley but Methodism out of back rooms and hidden halls and into the main stream of British life and history, out into the open, into the places where the multitude waited and where the battle had to be fought. It was George Whitefield who freed the Methodist evangel from the threat of four-wall littleness, from the stuffiness and complacency and inertia of a Church that had lost its touch with God and its common cause with mankind, and who made it, at the very moment it seemed ready to die, a Church of All Peoples, world-wide.

It may be that Whitefield is more potent in modern Methodism that John Wesley, though few Methodists seem aware of it. There is something virile, red-blooded, electric about Methodism; it smacks more of the battlefield than of the classroom. There is a shout in it. Or the echo of a shout, a great shout which came up from the collieries of Kingswood, and which has rolled like thunder across the years and the world. The shout of a massive man and massive spirit, who fought England's Armageddon in the streets and open fields, and brought off the victory.

IX

THE BATTLE FOR MISSIONS: WILLIAM CAREY

HE SAT with his mouth full of pegs, doing something to a run-down pair of shoes. That was his business. He was William Carey, Cobbler. "Second-Hand Shoes Bought and Sold," read the sign over his door. Before him, on his bench, lay a Greek grammar and a Bible; at his left elbow was a crude leathern globe, made of cobbler's leavings, with the continents and the nations of the world marked off in ink; on the wall behind him was a homemade map of the world, on which he had traced the travels of Captain Cook, England's idol of the hour. A pot of wax boiled on the pot-stove near the door.

When his mouth was free of the last peg, words came. *"Lego, legeis, legei."* That was from the Greek grammar: "I say, you say, he says." Or his hand spun the leathern globe: "China. Burma. Africa!" Or he stared at the map on the wall: "Captain Cook. Tahiti. Australia. Botany Bay!" Then some barefoot urchin would look in at the open door and laugh: "Hi there, Columbus." The dreamer would smile slowly and turn to his wax, which had boiled over.

To the citizens of Carey's town of Moulton, in Northamptonshire, the cobbler was a comic enigma. They couldn't understand him. Why should a shoemaker be studying Greek, and Latin, and French? (He acquainted himself with French in twenty-one days.) What had a plodder like him to do with globe-trotter Captain Cook? Why didn't he stick to his last? It didn't make sense to Moulton. It didn't make *much* sense to Carey himself. It seemed all tangled up, like a spool of thread unwound. Greek, Tahiti, Cook, New Testament, shoes, "I go, you go, he . . ." Tangled threads. Muddled dreams. Yet of all men in Moulton, Carey was the only one who was sure that the threads would untangle, would some day somehow be woven together into an intelligible pattern.

The old men of the town who sat and gossiped in his shop could never help him. They were forever arguing about the American Colonies, the rebels, the rascals who had fought the King and won. The old fellows couldn't believe it. George the Third had a hard time believing it, too. The King and the patriarchs of a thousand British Moultons puffed solemnly and ominously at their pipes when the news came that the rebel band at Yorktown, as the men of Cornwallis marched out to surrender, had played a tune called *The World Turned Upside Down.* Aye, upside down. But the cobbler let them puff and talk and fume; he heard little of it. His mind was bothered with a meaner surrender, the surrender of the Christian army to the gods of heathendom. He was worried about that thin red line of missionaries holding the line for Christ beyond the seas, who were struggling on after the Christians of the West had forsaken them. Christian missions had been dead, or as good as dead, for a century. Long after the old men had knocked out their pipes and gone home cursing Cornwallis, the cobbler would stand before his map, his Testament clasped in tight and bloodless fingers at his sturdy back, frowning, thinking of soles, and souls.

On Sundays he preached. He was good at that; he could pick words, could fit them into a discourse as delicately as he fitted lifts to the heel of a shoe. By 1786 he had become a regularly ordained minister, on the handsome salary of fifteen pounds per year. He did a great work. He had crowded altar-rails. But good as it was, there was something the matter with it. He had a far-away look in his eyes as he preached. He looked over the heads of his parishioners and penitents to . . . where, what, who? He talked a lot about foreign missions. Folks didn't just like that, for folks didn't just believe in foreign missions. There was enough to do right here at home, without sending money out to the "heathen." They were hard to convince, but Carey stuck to it.

He was asked to join the "preacher's meeting" of Northampton, and he joined. He was the junior member, the baby of a club of older clerics who were happy in their work, a work they had done in the same slow, easy, pacific pace for year on year. The same yesterday, today and forever. They were content with the snail-like progress of the army of the Lord; they were perfectly satisfied to work slowly, humbly, safely, taking no chances and winning one here, one there, tediously, for God. They were not enthusiastic. They were steady. Little wonder they were shocked the day the new junior member rose and read a paper on foreign missions! Carey asked brazenly ". . . Whether the command given to the Apostles, to teach all nations, was not obligatory on all succeeding ministers." The succeeding ministry of staid Northamptonshire rubbed its eyes and dug at its ears; it could have been no more shocked had the *enfant terrible* suggested that the King was not a Christian. There was a painful pause while the aged chairman gathered wits and breath enough to shout: *"Sit down, young man, sit down. You are a miserable enthusiast.* Certainly nothing can be done until another Pentecost. . . . When the Lord wants to convert the heathen He will do it without your help or mine." The junior member sat down.

But he sat down much as Galileo got up. Galileo, we are told, was forced to kneel before an arrogant and erring Church court and admit, against his mind and heart, that he was wrong in claiming that the earth moved around the sun. We are also told that the old scientist, awed but unbeaten, got to his feet again muttering under his breath, "Nevertheless, it moves." Carey was no more beaten than Galileo. He had been too long straightening out those tangled threads, too long dreaming of carrying the cross down the trail of Captain Cook. He knew now what he must do. And he knew too that he had a battle to fight, before he could do it. A battle with his own brothers of the cloth, who waited for another Pentecost. He hammered at them. He preached missions. He turned to use the help of the press, writing tracts and pamphlets. He talked into the small hours of the morning with anyone who would lend him an ear. He won over his first few sympathizers in pulpit and pew; he started a little group of tithers, who promised to give a penny a week to missions. (What miracles have been wrought in this world, on such pennies-a-week!) And some months later, in a little parlor in the town of Kettering, he pushed through the organization of "The Particular Baptist Society for Propagating the Gospel among the Heathen." It was the first society England had seen organized for such a purpose. It was a small society. There were only twelve in that parlor, but they were the successors of the Twelve in the Upper Room. Did they know it? And did they know that they were relighting the Protestant missionary torch after centuries of half-heartedness, under the spell of the cobbler of Moulton who was to be honored soon by the whole Protestant world as the founder and father of the modern Missions?

Carey went back to his shop in a fever of excitement, thinking of Tahiti, West Africa, Hawaii, Captain Cook. He forgot Captain Cook the day John Thomas crossed his path. John Thomas was Doctor Thomas, surgeon, lately medical missionary to India. Eccentricities and bad debts had just driven him from Calcutta, and he was in England now raising money to go back. He heard about the Society, and about William Carey; he hunted out the shoemaker and suggested that they pool what money they had, and book passage immediately for . . . India. A good ship, the British East Indiaman *Oxford*, was pulling at her anchor off the coast, ready to go. Carey fell on his neck and kissed him, packed his bags, held a futile argument with his disagreeing wife, and went (with her) aboard the ship. Eastward ho! He was on his way.

No, not quite. The Captain of the *Oxford* put him off the ship. He put off all the missionaries, all their families and their luggage and their hopes, for someone had whispered in his ear that this man Thomas was a bad one, head over heels in debt, with an evil reputation. Someone had also whispered to him that the British East Indian Company, owners of the *Oxford*, wanted no more missionaries in India. They were a troublesome lot, said the Company, forever stirring up the natives. Chaplains for the British Army were all right, but preachers for the natives . . . no! The Company, you see, was in India for what it could get out of India, out of the natives, and a native with an "exaggerated" idea of his own rights or importance wasn't easy to deal with. So when the Company objected, that settled it. Carey and

Thomas would never sail to India under the British flag. They went ashore in a dory as the *Oxford* slipped off into the fog. Beaten again, this time by the lords of commerce, who did not believe in foreign missions.

Carey was disconsolate. Mrs. Carey, the unconvinced, was almost glad. The Particular Baptist Society for Propagating the Gospel among the Heathen vowed it was undone, finished. John Thomas developed a sulk, and went down to a water-front coffee-house to sulk it out. He inquired idly of the sailors in the place about other ships outfitting for India, but he got no favorable clew. When he had abandoned hope and paid his score, a waiter came over to his table and slipped into his hand a greasy, finger-marked card on which some careful, unknown friend had written: "A Danish East Indiaman. No. 10 Cannon Street." Posterity has sinned in losing that card; it was important. It meant that Carey and the surgeon could go, after all; go, under the Danish flag. At dawn on the thirteenth of June, in 1792, they stood together on the deck of the *Kron Princessa Maria*, peering back at the dark blot of land that was England. Carey never saw England again. He wouldn't have cared, even had he known that. He was anxious to see India, to begin his battle in earnest. It was five months before he saw India, five months before his ship coasted down the Bay of Bengal, passing another ship, England-bound, on whose decks walked Lord Cornwallis. Yes, the same Cornwallis who had heard the band play at Yorktown, and who was now quitting as Governor-General of India, the last of the historic triumvirate of Clive, Hastings and Cornwallis. They passed each other in the Bay: the haughty aristocrat who represented the end of an epoch of Empire written in blood and cruelty, and a cobbler tied to a sickly wife, whose sole helper was a discredited physician with a lot of bad debts, but who with these was about to do for India and the Indian and the East what Paul had done for Rome and the Gentiles.

And what was this India he was "taking over" from Cornwallis? It was an ancient India, an old mother. Mother of men: among her ancients were the forebears of the Indo-European, the Roman and the Greek. An immensely wealthy mother, India, a domain vaster and richer than Rome, was the home of the Kohinoor diamond and the rich Himalayas. An intensely fertile mother, secreting in her bosom fortunes in silver, copper, gold, and rubies, pouring out of a great natural cornucopia showers of precious sandalwood and teak, rice, wheat, cotton, indigo, tea and jute. Chu Chin Chow might have envied the wealth of her princes, living, living yet, in barbaric splendor, in billion-dollar pageantry and panoply and waste. India was mother to the arts and culture; there was a tool factory in Madras while there were still cave-men in Britain, bathrooms in 3500 B.C. such as have not yet been surpassed in Manhattan, startling sculpture and miracles in jewelry and ceramics, artists who worked in chiseled ivory, miniature paintings, wood carving, fine cloth ("calico" comes from "Calicut"), builders who created Taj Mahal and Peacock Throne and Akbar's Tomb and Delhi's Fort. Builders of ships; builders of great industries; engineers, bankers, merchant-princes. Linguists who put speech on the tongues of men: here was born Sanscrit; here came into being the immortal Ramayana, the Mahabharata, Bhagavad-Gita, sacred Vedas, and Upanashads, mathematics, philosophy, profound metaphysics. Here was the mother-land of religion. Mark Twain said that India was a religious millionaire, with "a thousand religions and

three million gods, and she worships all of them." They had
their religious Book of Manu long, long before the Wise Men
reached Bethlehem; they knew the gentle Buddha and the less
gentle Mohammed; they listened to the teachings of Kabir,
Nanak, and Chitanya.

But all this wealth meant little to India; this was a robbed
and devastated land, victim of centuries of foreign plun-
derers. Over her had swept the armies and the merchants of
Alexander the Great, Mohammed, the Great Moguls, the
Portuguese, Danes, Dutch, British and French, all too often
aided by native Indian princes themselves. Carnage was
king, and the horn of plenty was split open by one sword
after another. It was long and it was bloody. When the
British won at Plassy, the Indian settled down to a rule of
tyranny and bloodshed under Clive. Treaties were made
solemnly and broken with a laugh. Treaties were forged.
Hindu rulers were forced to make "presents" to their white
masters at gun-point; tribute was exacted to the tune of
millions. Princes were played against princes, their subjects
annihilated and their treasure-vaults smashed open. Exces-
sive taxes were levied and tax-defaulters were exposed in
cages open to the sun; rebels were hanged. Fortunes were
paid for quarter and quarter was then denied; fathers sold
their sons to pay their taxes; when the flow from the golden
reservoir slacked, torture which would have honored mon-
sters was employed. Yet when Clive went home to England
to answer charges to an outraged homeland, he remarked to
Parliament: "When I think of the marvelous riches of that
country, and the comparatively small part which I took
away, I am astonished at my own moderation." After Clive
came Hastings, living in open adultery, fearless statesman
and unscrupulous trickster, burning countless Indian vil-

lages, killer with a heart as stone-cold as his sword. And then Cornwallis, who, to give him his due, was better. These were the white rulers who opposed the coming of the missionary. These were the ones to whom India had bowed in deep disdain:

> "She let the legions thunder past,
> Then plunged in thought again."

India ignored the future, fearing it; she clung to the past, loving it. As for the present, she just suffered through it. She did not even look up when Carey came. What was one more Englishman?

Last but hardly least, the Moulton cobbler found in India a cruel heritage of handicap. These religions and gods, for instance: they were inoculating India with a spiritual and social poison as deadly as the venom secreted in the fangs of the Indian cobra. Carey knew of the great car of Juggernaut lumbering across the land, and of frenzied devotees throwing themselves blindly to be crushed beneath its wheels; he knew of young men and maidens, decked with flowers and singing, slain in the temples to appease the gods; he heard of worshipers stoning themselves publicly to death, of men thrusting iron hooks through their backs and held suspended in midair at the "swinging festivals." Millions bowed to sacred monkeys, sacred cows, sacred snakes. Multitudes had no other god than a log of wood, no savior but the Ganges. Gods, gods, gods: they were gods of clay, and at their feet lay India, prostrate.

Brahmanism was mothering caste, dividing all India into four divisions: Brahmans and Kshatriyas, Vishayas and Sudras (priests and warriors, husbandmen and laborers.) Below these favored four were the miserable pariah, the outcaste, the untouchable, the hopeless who dwelt at the bottom of the pit. Their clothes were rags, their food was carrion. Should a caste man come within sixty-four feet of them, that man must go quickly to be "purified," maybe in the Ganges, the holiest and the dirtiest river in the world. In South India they might not visit the temples, nor walk the streets without sweeping the ground behind them with a brush. That was caste; that *is* caste, yet today, mothered and guarded by Hinduism, the faith of millions that has never lifted a finger to help its adherents out of the mire, that has maimed and crippled and blighted the happiness of one of the richest, noblest people on God's earth. There are even some non-Hindus who like it, who say, "Why not leave the native alone?"

They were burning widows in India when Carey stepped ashore. Suttee was a religious duty. Girl brides and old widows were bound to the bodies of their dead husbands, held down by long poles in the fire. Or a widow might be buried alive, sitting at the bottom of a pit with the corpse of her mate in her arms, while her own children threw in the dirt and trampled it tighter and tighter about her head until she died. What of it? What was a woman, anyway? She was a necessary evil, created by Brahma only that men might have sons. Fit only for marriage, she might be married off by her father at eight, ten, twelve years of age to a man twice, thrice her age; failing marriage, she might become a temple prostitute!

This was the India the cobbler faced; an India mothering wealth, beauty, culture, art, architecture, caste, superstition, suttee, squalor, oppression, ignorance; she gave fairy-palaces to the rich few, horror and hopelessness to the nine-tenths who lived in hard-scrabble poverty on the land, whose lives here were a choice between famine in the days of draught and flood in the days of rain, and who in the next world might choose between being transmigrated into a snake or a jungle-flower. Carey set himself to fight that. He faced it almost alone, with a startling lack of school-education and an over-abundance of Christian courage, with the most passively resistant people on the face of the earth before him and the luke-warmness of England and the Church behind him. He squared his shoulders, and settled down to the battle upon which depended the fate of Christ in the East, the fate of the East itself.

He started preaching. He preached in the streets until he could scrape enough together to build a little Baptist Church. He preached for seven years before he got his first native convert. (Did a prominent American minister, just yesterday, say that preaching was being wasted, that we should have a moratorium from sermons? Carey never thought so, though it took him seven years.) He studied the languages and the dialects of the land, learned to speak and write them. He ran out of money, took a job in an indigo factory to keep himself and his family alive, pored over his language-books in the dead of night while jackals howled and tigers prowled in the brush of the Dinajpoor swamps at his door, and "holy" men barked like dogs in the street. His child died. His wife was a burden. He sent hopeful, optimistic letters to England, telling his friends that all was well. He got pessimistic, depressing letters back from England, telling him that money was short at home, and that they didn't see how they could help him any longer. Times were hard in England! Aye, said the cobbler, and times were harder than hard in India. He went on as though all the wealth of the Empire was at his beck and call. He fought on, when even a fool might have known the battle was lost. He completed a translation of the New Testament, setting a standard of prose and an arrangement of Sanscrit borrowings which has affected Bengali prose to this hour. He and Surgeon John Thomas tied Krishna Pal to a tree and prayed for him while they set his broken leg; while the bone healed, Carey made a Christian of Krishna. Krishna was baptized in the River Hoogly, and he was invited to dinner with the missionaries. He came, sat down to eat beef with foreigners, and thereby struck a hard blow at an old and paralyzing doctrine of Ahisma.

At the height of his lonely labors, word came to Carey that four new British missionaries had come to India (on an American ship), and were locating at Danish Serampore, near Calcutta. He threw up his job in the indigo factory and went to Serampore, where he shook hands with the newcomers, Joshua Marshman, William Ward, and their wives. Carey, Marshman and Ward! Why are they so little known, so forgotten? Why did Kipling never write of them? Kipling, with his "soldiers three," whose chief purpose in India was to "keep their accouterments spotlessly clean, to refrain from getting drunk more often than is necessary, to obey their superiors and to pray for a war." Why did Kipling immortalize this unholy three, who came to India with guns in their hands? And why did he ignore the holier three, Carey and Marshman and Ward, who came as the ambassadors of Brother Christ to strike off chains and set India free?

Marshman was an educator; his forte was schools. His wife, Hannah, started a school for girls, a dangerous, unheard-of thing for anyone to do, in view of what India thought of the woman and the girl; it was the first of those schools which have taught a finer conception of womanhood,

THE BATTLE FOR MISSIONS: WILLIAM CAREY

in which the Christian teacher lifted the Indian woman to
a nobler status and estate. Ward was a printer; through
his presses poured a stream of written words which became
paving-stones in the highway over which all the missionaries who followed him were to take their way. Ward printed
what Carey translated, an almost lifework in itself. For
Carey the translator was tireless; his translations came so
fast that people began to call him the Wyclif of the East.
That was high praise for one who but a few years before
had been the butt of jokes in Moulton, but it was praise
well earned. He not only translated or guided the trans-
lating of Indian classics, preserving thereby a wealth of
ancient prose and poetry, but he also created dictionaries
and grammars, so that even the humblest and the lowest
might read. He threw open the pages of the Bible to all
India: he is responsible for thirty-one million pages of the
Old and New Testaments in the languages of the East. Before he died, *he had translated the Bible or parts of it into
forty dialects and languages.* He made the Bible accessible
to three hundred million human beings. And he edited three
volumes of the Ramayana.

He was educator to India. He fathered schools and built
a college. He saw that if Christ were to live in India, He
must live through native Christian preacher-teachers who
could reach the Indian heart and mind as no European
could hope to reach them. So he built Serampore, a college
for the training of a native ministry. That college was the
effort of his life. Now that he has gone on, it remains, im-
mortalizing him. Through its doors yearly comes a trained
ministry, thanking God for him.

And he was scientist. As a boy in England he collected
seeds and butterflies and flowers. As a man he put away his

[133]

childish collecting and turned his mind to the relation of botany to faith, of soils and plants and agriculture to the life of India. He wrote home to England: "Do send me a few tulips, daffodils, lilies." Later he asked for acorns, that he might plant oaks at Serampore. He planted a garden, and it became the most famous botanical experiment-station in India. He catalogued plant and animal life, told India what would grow best and where, founded the Agricultural and Horticultural Society of India and furnished with it the model for the great British Society which came later. He offered medals and cash for the growing of better coffee and cotton and European fruits; he was elected to the Asiatic Society in recognition of his work. He stimulated the manufacture of a cheese the equal of any made in Cheshire, the growing of vegetables as fine as any ever grown in England; he held a food show in Calcutta. He went to a people ignorant of scientific methods of farming, living by the million on farms a western farmer would never look at twice, plundered by a foreign government and forced into slavery by their own money-lenders; he taught them to improve and "crop" their land, and he made them plant trees from English seeds and acorns, trees that would catch and hold and store up the water so sorely needed by their thirsty soil. He talked to farmers of fallow earth and fertile earth. He manufactured indigo, and printing type, started the first newspaper and set up the first steam-engine in India. And there are still some people who think there is something effeminate, something "sissy" about the missionary!

He was philanthropist, benefactor, humanitarian. He saw a widow burned, went home sick at the sight, so sick that his servant asked, "Art thou bitten by a serpent, sahib?"

No, not bitten by a serpent, but stung to action. He went at suttee hammer and tongs; he never let up until he had started a movement against it that ended in its abolishment. He enlisted the aid of Indians and Englishmen; commissioned to investigate and report on suttee by the British Government, he filed a report with Lord Bentinck, finest of India's governors, that resulted in a law abolishing widow-burning forever. He reported on infant sacrifice. He had seen babies exposed in baskets in the trees, exposed to the pitiless sun and deadly white ants; he had seen them torn from their mothers and thrown to alligators and sharks. He protested to the English. He sent in another report. Infant sacrifice stopped. Carey stopped it. He fought the burning-ghats, and lost; the old and the dying are still carried to the shores of the Ganges, and their deaths hastened. The custom persists. So does the Christian objection. He fought the self-inflicted cruelty of the swinging-festivals, and he lost again. Some still are held in India. The hero in this stranger-than-fiction story did not always win. He saw a leper burned at Calcutta in 1812, burned alive, by his mother and sister; Carey did not rest until he had brought about the establishment of a leper hospital in Calcutta, the first in India. Fit finale, this, to his works of benevolence. Lepers in India now need not hide themselves, nor cry the bloodcurdling "Unclean, unclean!" of the mother of Ben Hur. There are havens of refuge for them now, refuges, colonies, hospitals; doctors, nurses go across the seas from England and America to treat and maybe cure them. Fit finale, for soon after this, Carey died. Died no longer a joke, a "tub-preacher," a "consecrated cobbler," but Professor of Sanscrit in a government college, honored by the very government that had tried to keep him from preaching in

India! He died, but the good he did lives after him. Seeds blew from his garden on the wings of the wind, taking root in far-off, unexpected places. Seeds from his great fertile heart blew too, taking root, blossoming. . . .

It might have happened some other way, through some other man or men. It didn't. It happened because a Moulton cobbler fought alone to make it happen, when even his own tried to tell him he was mad.

X

THE BATTLE WITH SOCIETY

GOD'S struggle with Society began in the Garden of Eden; the first sermon of the Social Gospel was preached by the Lord God as He walked in the Garden in the cool of the day. It was a three-word sermon, preached to a congregation of two. It was this: "Where art thou?" Where art thou, thou two sinning members of the first society? Where art thou, sinning and shamed and shunning the Lord? Why have ye fallen so? Why hide ye in the shadows, dreading His presence? It is the eternally tireless God on the hunt for eternally shamed and sinning woman and man.

The second sermon was preached beyond the bounds of Eden. There was a smaller audience; an audience of one; a murderer. There was a longer sermon. Five words. The Lord God said to Cain, "Where is Abel thy brother?" Thy brother! Is he lost, hungry, oppressed, naked, sick, imprisoned, dead? Cain, trying to excuse himself, put upon the lips of society the unmanly, unholy excuse it has used ever since that day: "Am I my brother's keeper?" He got his answer, an answer that should have staggered him and silenced us: "Thy brother's blood crieth unto me from the ground."

Unofficially, the battle began there, with Adam and Adam's son Cain. Officially, it began with Moses, in a brickyard. Not in lazy, easy Eden, but in the roar of a strike in Egypt. Moses has been described as history's first successful

labor agitator, the first great strike-leader among Christ's
people. The description is correct. He agitated not for more
pay or shorter hours; he was in the hire of no labor union,
no political party, no social theorist. He agitated for God.
He sought a more abundant life for the children of God.
His drive, his impulse, his passion were neither social nor
economic, but religious. He sought to drive from his people
the lusts of Mammon in order that they might live in the
love of God. His cry, his sermon was: "Let my people go!"
Go, to Canaan. Go, back to God.

In these three men and movements we have the genesis
of Christianity's struggle for a better society, a better world.
God and Adam and Cain and Moses: these were the advance
scouts of the battle. "Where art thou . . . Thy brother's
blood . . . Let my people go . . ." this was the good old religion, the faith of our fathers. This was a *social* religion.
It has always been social. It has begun but never stopped
with the individual. It has always been brother-minded; if
there is any one word that describes it, that word is "Others."
It has cherished always the hope of a saved world for saved
men to live in, a Kingdom-of-God sort of world, where God
reigned as truly as He reigned in Heaven. Follow its course
from Eden. Follow it as it issues from Eden's gate and
struggles for survival through the wild days of Enoch and
Noah and Abraham and Joseph; its struggle all through
those days was a struggle not to protect a chosen few, but
to bring more and more to live together in peace and love.
Follow it with Moses through the wilderness; look sharply
at the Ten Commandments, and see how largely they were
written for the protection of the exploited, the slaves, the
strangers, even the dumb beasts of burden; see here the
beginning of the eight-hour law and the Sunday closing law.

Others! See God scourging social and political sin with Elijah on Carmel, with Nehemiah and Jeremiah. Behold the eighth-century prophets scorning holiness in the abstract and dealing in definite, current, concrete social situations, religious reformers calling for a social cleansing in order that individuals might find it possible to live according to the dictates of their God. Hear old Amos crying, "They sold the righteous for silver, and the poor for a pair of shoes;" that was a later Moses crying, "Let my [poor] people go." Hear Hosea, speaking for God: "I desired mercy and not sacrifice; and the knowledge of God more than burnt offerings." Hear Micah: "And what does the Lord require of thee, but to do justly, and to love mercy, and to walk humbly with thy God." Thus was Christianity brother-minded, social-minded, even before it *was* Christianity!

Then came Jesus, preaching the Kingdom of God. Jesus read the prophets, knew them, loved them, quoted them. He took up the battle where they left it. He was painfully particular about current conditions. Painfully particular, and scathingly social. "He that hath two coats, let him share with him that hath none; and he that hath food, let him do likewise . . . Love thy neighbor . . . Do unto others as ye would that others . . . When ye pray, say *our* . . ." He talked of feeding the hungry, clothing the naked, helping alien Samaritans, visiting the prisoner. He spoke for a neglected childhood: "Suffer the little children . . ." He despised the craving for wealth which choked God in the soul of man: "Sell all that thou hast . . ." He loathed war: "Put up again thy sword . . ." He served all men, and not a few: Nicodemus the scholar, Zaccheus the despised tax-collector, Mary the Magdalene, publicans, princes, sinners, Gadarene demoniacs and the woman taken in adultery. Kings have gone down on their knees to him; the common people have heard him gladly. Jesus served all. Jesus was brother-at-large to humanity. He sought first to save the individual soul, and that was a means to an end. The end was the Kingdom of God, a social community, a community of the righteous living the good life before they died, here and now, on this earth. He fought poverty, war, oppression, every inch of the way from the manger to the cross.

After Jesus, the deluge. For a while the first Christians were so much fearful dynamite beneath the surface of the Roman state, boring from within to build a Kingdom of Love on a soil hostile and bloody with brother-blood. There were deacons in the New Testament Church, charged with the care of the widow, the orphan, the sick and the poor. There was a short-lived experiment in Christian communism, in which at least a part of them "sold their possessions and goods, and parted them to all men, as every man had need." There was at least a communism of religious and social interest among them, from the beginning. But as the years wore on and the hope of Christ's return was deferred and postponed again and again and again, they began to lift their eyes and thoughts from the woes of earth to the raptures of Heaven. They became other-worldly; they neglected this world for the next. Their ears grew deaf to the cries of the widowed and the orphaned and the sick as they sang louder and louder of streets of gold and gates of jasper and pearl in the glory-land beyond. Their hope of building the kingdom here, on this earth, waned; what they needed were more men in white to bring them to their senses with the admonition of those men in white in early Acts: "Why stand ye gazing up into heaven?" But there were no such men. They stood on tiptoe trying to look through the windows of Heaven while their feet walked on an earth stained with blood and trembling with poverty and pain. Time came when the Church dropped its sackcloth for royal purple; when, after Constantine, it acquired power and pelf undreamed of, dignity and respectability and rich royal robes. When Rome fell, the popes took over; the popes aped the Cæsars, sat on thrones, borrowed the forms of the Roman state and ruled with an iron hand. The Church threw off the democracy and brotherhood of the first Church first for an oligarchy and then for a monarchy. There came tyrant popes and some good ones, all with their henchmen far and wide to enforce obedience to the rules of the Holy See and to stamp out whatever was left of democracy and the love of liberty. By the time the fifth century arrived, the Church was the largest landowner in the world, the lord of earth and the keeper of the keys to Heaven. Then Augustine arrived on the scene and wrote his *City of God,* and this Church which had started as an agency for the building of the Kingdom came to think that it was the Kingdom itself. Thus it went through the ages called Dark; scholarly speculation became more important than social salvation; the scholars debated furiously over how many angels could dance on the point of a needle while the dark angels of hunger and woe had their own way with the people in the street. No longer need the Church say, "Silver and gold have I none . . ." Neither had it power to say to the sick of earth, "Take up thy bed and walk."

Yet even through that Medieval darkness, Christianity was social and brother-minded at heart, though the Church as an organization had become something else. Through this dark shambles there were schools, teachers bearing torches in the night: the only schools were church-schools.

In this age were established the first orphanages, the first homes for the aged, and the first crude hospitals for the sick. Even while the organization was piling up privilege and profit and lands and profits and rent, the Christ-spirit lying so chained at the heart of it managed to carry on the battle for the benighted. The coffers of the Vatican may have been bursting, but the Waldensian movement was abroad, led by men who washed their hands of wealth and who went to live with the common people. Some of the clergy may have become despots, but little St. Francis was out on the road, calling the Church back to the powerful penury of the Christ, begging food in the hut of the peasant and loving even the wild beast. Mammon may have been the power behind the throne at St. Peter's, but Arnold of Brescia and John Wyclif fought him, in the name of a common humanity and a common brother, Christ. Even now, Christianity was fostering learning and relieving distress, when no other institution in the world thought of doing it.

When the curtain rises on the next act, we find Martin Luther and John Calvin on the stage, laying their Reformation axes to the roots of that old order and bringing it down, clearing the way for a rebirth of the kingdom hope' and the old passion for a saved society for saved men to live in. These reformers were no democrats, yet they cleared the way for democracy; they were no economists nor sociologists, yet they set free the Christian mind and conscience and encouraged man to build a new and more just economy, a new and more Christian society. They left the world with that hope, but they also left it in the throes of a theological argument that was to last for four hundred years; it took us that long to formulate and separate our creeds, to become Calvinists, Lutherans, Baptists, Methodists, Presbyterians and Congregationalists. From 1500 to 1800, the Gospel was more individual than social; we talked much of natural rights and almost never of social structure; we were busy clothing our faith in the habiliments of creed, while humanity shivered in the bitter cold of a quite heartless and careless world, with no coat at all. People were hungry. They were thirsty. Three-quarters or more of them were poor. Crime was rampant. Men drank themselves into insensibility to forget their troubles or died like sheep in the wars of their lords. They cried for bread, and got stones. Suddenly, it happened. There came a lull in the theologian's debating, and in the lull Christianity heard a babel of voices that had been swelling up for centuries. Suddenly, Christianity changed front. It heard those voices. It rediscovered humanity, and girded itself for a hundred-years war against such a society and such an economics. It was the nineteenth century.

Christianity could not very well help but hear it, hear these cries, these moans. For the nineteenth century was a noisy, clattering century. On the horizon was the smoke of ten thousand factories, the spawn of the Industrial Revolution. The ear of everyone was deafened by the clang of the machine, and the eyes and lungs of men were filled with the soot and smoke and cinder of the mill. Slums grew like mushrooms in the industrial centers. Rather, like poisonous toadstools, for they were unhealthy and unchristian and unclean, sewers of sin, pouring forth across society a stream of crime and physical disease. The life of every city, every nation, was in a poisoned state. Mankind was unhealthy, untidy, a huddled, chaotic Donnybrook Fair fumbling for security and finding none, crying for peace, peace, and finding no peace. Moan on moan the babel mounted; out of the murk and the confusion came a new host of the hungry and the sick and the chained, putting an end to the creedal debate with a piteous cry: "Help us, Christian! If you ever thought of others, think of us, now. If ever you heard your brother's blood crying to you . . ." And Christianity realized that while it might be well to save a soul, that a soul would have a battle against impossible odds to remain saved in such a world, such an unchristian environment as this; that while you might get a drunkard to sign a pledge, it would be hard for him to keep it with a saloon on every corner; that while it might be good to have a Sunday school, it was bad to have a mill in which the child was worked by a profiteering mill-owner into such a state of exhaustion that he couldn't keep his eyes open in Sunday school; that while it was good to think of peace and good-will at Christmas, it was blasphemy to go to war the day after Christmas. And so Christianity turned to answer the cry of the stricken world with a new tactic; it turned from the old method of snatching a few wrecks, here and there, from the ravages of unchristian society, and struck at the root causes of the wrecking. It refused to be any longer an ambulance plodding along in the wake of disaster, and set itself to correct those forces and influences which made the disaster possible. It was to be a long fight. We are in the midst of it, in 1937.

Out of the jungles of Africa came the cry of the Negro in chains. Slavery! Grim slave-ships, which should have been flying the Black Roger at their mast-heads, toiled up the middle passage with black men, women and children moaning in their holds, with dead black bodies floating in their wakes, food for the trailing sharks. Africa shook its shackled wrists at the white man and cried, "Let my people go." A Moses in England heard the cry, an Evangelical who loved his fellow man. William Wilberforce, M. P., fired by John Wesley (as indeed most of the leaders in the early fight for a Christian social order were fired), set himself against the institution of slavery, gave twenty-five years of his life to the job of scuttling the slave-ship. Three days before he died, friends came to his bedside to tell him that his law had passed Parliament, and that never again would there be a slave chained in the shadow of the Union Jack. Thirty years later (thanks to the Quaker and Abraham Lincoln) the last slave went free in America, dropping his chains on a soil stained a horrible red with his white brother's blood. Slavery is gone today. It was a germ that thrived in darkness, and it simply could not live in the blazing light of Christianity.

Out of the factories and mills of the nineteenth and twentieth centuries came the lament of the laborer. The laborers were men, women, children. They were the new slaves, in machine-made chains. A young, blue-blooded lord in England was the pioneer in the fight to rescue them. Lord Shaftesbury went into the factories to see how things were; he found that "Day and night the machinery was kept going; one gang of children working it by day, and another set by night, while, in times of pressure, the same children were kept working day and night by remorseless taskmasters." He went down into the mines, and found women and girls crawling through shafts, on their hands and knees, shafts that were as narrow and wet as sewers, chained to coal-cars, crawling in the dark, often, until the last hour of pregnancy! He followed little chimney-sweeps in the street: "They began the day's work at four, three, even two in the morning; they were half stifled by the hot sulphurous air in the flues; they would often get stuck in the chimney, and faint from the effects of terror, exhaustion and foul air . . . they were sometimes killed outright. . . ." He stood up in Parliament to fight for that laborer, with all that cruelty and injustice flaming from his eyes. He shamed England. He made Englishmen see their brothers, their sisters, their children. Out of his fourteen-year battle came laws which outlawed such conditions, such slavery. England remembers him not as a rich young ruler but as "the working man's friend."

He was the first of a new order of Christians who championed labor. After him came the Christian Socialists, Kingsbury and Maurice, Scott Holland, Thomas Hughes and John Ludlow, who carried on when he was gone. Then Keir Hardie, who swore that if he could live again he would give his life to the preaching of the Gospel of Jesus Christ, and who founded the British Labour Party, the most potent political organization of modern times. He and those champions of labor who followed him did not always have the help they should have had from organized Christianity, for there were mill-owners and industrialists in the pews; but they had, and they knew that they had, the help of the Christ. But the Church may have helped more than we sometimes think. When Terence V. Powderly, Grand Master Workman of the Knights of Labor, said in 1892, "You can count on the ends of your fingers all the clergymen who take any interest in the labor problem," the editor of a Christian magazine promptly furnished a list of one hundred and twenty-two who are interested in a most determined way. When the Federal Council of the Churches of Christ in America was established in 1908, its most significant act was the drawing up of a "Social Creed of the Churches," which demanded the abolition of child labor, safety devices on factory machinery, a minimum wage, the right of collective bargaining, and a new distribution of profit and property. When a steel strike broke out in Pittsburgh in 1919, it was Bishop Francis J. McConnell who headed a committee to investigate the causes of the strike, and who submitted a report which is directly responsible for the eight-hour day in steel. When the accusation came again that the Church was not interested in labor, Charles Stelzle arranged an interchange of delegates between Church and union meetings, and a Labor Temple came into being in New York. A new emphasis took hold of the pulpit; no longer do we hear ministers pleading with labor to accept a dollar a day as their "lot"; now we find them on picket-lines. No longer do we find them turning a cold shoulder, as in Shaftesbury's day, on child labor; the Federal Council leads the fight today for a Child Labor Amendment in the Constitution of the United States.

Out of the slums came the cry of the poor, and again the Christ-spirit answered with a fight for the elimination of poverty. Shaftesbury started that, too. He went into the homes of the poor, found them filthy, too nauseatingly filthy to enter, found horrors as bad as the horrors of the middle passage, found doctors writing their prescriptions outside the doors; found the slum crawling with vermin and festering crime. He fought stubbornly against the low wages that produced the demand for such cheap and dirty living; he died, and the conditions were still there. After him, General William Booth went down into the slum, preached and prayed and told the world that he almost despaired of the poor ever being "as well cared for as horses." Down into the slum, down to the haunts of the children of poverty went young British scholars, to found Toynbee Hall; down

[147]

to the slum went Jane Addams to found Hull House; down there went Graham Taylor of the Chicago Theological Seminary, to found Chicago Commons. These men and women of the classes who went to live with the masses stirred the social consciousness of the churches. Aided by the two leading Social Gospel preachers, Washington Gladden of Columbus and Professor Rauschenbush of Rochester, they awakened within us a new sense of our responsibility; they made us see that while poverty may come of man's frailty, the slum and the hovel come of man's deliberation. They began to make us see that the condition of the poor is the fault of all of us; that it was unchristian as well as inhuman for us to allow a few men to hold all the wealth, while multitudes cried for bread. Less and less often did we hear sermons on "poverty as a blessing in disguise"; more and more did we hear sermons in which poverty was pictured as the direct result of man's greed and blundering. Today the pulpit is insisting that we share the good things of life; that we have no right to "make money according to the laws of business and spend it according to the laws of God"; that God should govern both getting and spending. Today the fight for the poor man is our most decisive battle. Today, while we still send out Thanksgiving baskets, there is an increasing tendency to ask, "Why are these baskets necessary at all?"

Out of the alley grog-shop and the rich man's saloon came the moans of the slaves of Barleycorn. Alcohol! This was a battle already old when John Wesley appeared to fight gin-drinking. For years after him, even ministers drank; ecclesiastical gatherings in the American Colonies often ended with "alcoholic refreshment." But that stopped in short order once the magnitude of the evil of alcohol became apparent to the Churches, and long before the late nineteenth century, the Church and the saloon knew that they had in each other a deadly enemy. Temperance was preached ardently before Wesley died, through the medium of lecture, tract and pulpit; this was the drip, drip, drip on the stone. By 1869 there was a Prohibition Party in the United States; by 1874, there was a Women's Christian Temperance Union with a Frances E. Willard at its head. Twenty years later we had a Wayne B. Wheeler and an Anti-Saloon League. By 1918 there was an Eighteenth Amendment, and now there is Repeal. What there may be tomorrow—who knows? Only this is certain: that tomorrow the Christian conscience of the nation will probably hate alcohol as much as it does today; tomorrow it will be fighting alcohol not just because it is alcohol, but because of its evil tide it brings in poverty, and crime, and suffering, and moral insensibility, and religious inertia. If Barleycorn overcomes every other enemy, he will still have the Church.

Out of the state-house came the stench of political corruption. Politics meant plunder. The Church, objecting to that, was told to mind her own business. But the Church believed that the welfare and the cleanliness of the race was as much her business as the politicians', and she proceeded forthwith to mix religion with politics, in a manner most disturbing to the Bill Tweeds and Boss Nashes. Doctor Parkhurst invaded the Bowery in 1892, and on Sunday told his Madison Avenue congregation of the alliance he had found there between corrupt New York politics and commercialized vice; he tied Tammany Hall fast to the saloon. There was some explaining, some hectic scrambling to get out of the preacher's way . . . and a wholesale cleaning of the political household. There are many Parkhursts today; they are in every church, in every denomination, insisting

[149]

that inasmuch as better politics depends upon a better type of character, and that inasmuch as character-building is a function of religion, then religion and politics are inextricably bound together.

Last but not least there is war. Out of the graves of the million, million, million soldier dead, from Cain to the Marne, came the voice of the dead killed in war. Our brother's blood cried to us from the good earth, demanding that we dig graves for soldier dead no more, that we beat our swords into plowshares and our spears into pruning-hooks. War once seemed to us inevitable, somehow glorious although somehow unchristian, an evil we were unable to stop, and that we'd better make up our minds to tolerate. But the Church, across the last hundred years, has slowly been making up her mind to something else. Gradually the conviction deepened that war was not at all inevitable, but an international crime deliberately fostered and encouraged by men who expected to profit by it; that war was not made by one man's country against another, but by governments, and that if the governed were to insist long enough and strenuously enough, the governments would find another way of settling their disputes. We looked upon the bodies of youth mashed in front-line trenches like so many rotten vegetables, and we failed to see anything glorious in it. We have come to despise the war-profiteer and the merchants of death who traffic in arms and the paraphernalia of war. So far has our war on war gone that it would be like searching for the proverbial needle in the proverbial haystack to find a church daring to put in a good word in defense of Mars. Never before has the Christian conscience been so aroused and determined to outlaw war. And never before, alas, has there been such need for such a conscience. Today there are forty million men in the world under arms. That is a threat of world-proportions, a threat the Church must meet, or go down in a welter of blood. In view of what has happened to one Church in Spain, we know now that either the Church of Christ will wipe out war, or be wiped out by war.

So has the battle gone for a hundred years and more, since John Wesley told us to "beware of a solitary religion." So has our thinking and our action changed as we have striven to make of it a religion dominating all of life and not a part of it. There have been great victories and stinging defeats as we have battled poverty and alcohol, slavery, greed, graft and ignorance, and there will be more. The fight has only begun: when all has been said, it must be admitted that we are but semi-Christian, socially, today. We have Christianized the home, the school, the Church; we have crossed swords with the glaring evils of yesterday. Today we have leveled our lances against Mammon in industry and Mars in war. Tomorrow . . . well, tomorrow there will be new enemies, new battles. We shall never cease approaching decisive battles, for we shall never have a Christianity content with things as they are. As Edwin Markham reminds us:

> "Always there shall be vision for the heart,
> The press of endless passion, every goal
> A traveler's tavern, whence we must depart
> On new divine adventures of the soul."

THE END